# enrich-e-matics

### 3rd EDITION

## BOOK 3

**Anne Joshua**

MA, Dip Ed (Syd); MSc (Oxon)

# enrich-e-matics
## 3rd EDITION

## Dear Teachers, Students and Parents,

Thank you for purchasing *Enrich-e-matics 3rd Edition*. This is the third of a series of six books designed to develop and enrich students' problem-solving skills. *Enrich-e-matics 3rd Edition* deepens students' mathematical concepts and encourages flexibility of thinking along with a willingness to tackle challenging and fascinating problems. The series was originally designed to cater for the mathematically able student but was also found to be a useful tool for all schools wishing to strengthen their students' mathematical understanding.

## What is different about *Enrich-e-matics 3rd Edition*?

*Enrich-e-matics 3rd Edition* is much more than a collection of puzzles and difficult problems. The exercises are *graded*. Concepts and strategies are developed throughout the series to provide for a systematic development of problem-solving and mathematical ability.

The exercises and activities have been grouped into mathematics strands—**Number, Patterns & Algebra, Chance & Data, Measurement, Space** and **Working Mathematically**—with hundreds of new problems added. This allows students and teachers to work systematically through a number of similar problems focusing on one area of mathematics. It also allows flexibility of programming so that material from different strands can be integrated. The strand is indicated on each page by an icon. Themes are introduced and developed throughout the series. The answers for all problems are included in a removable section at the back of the book.

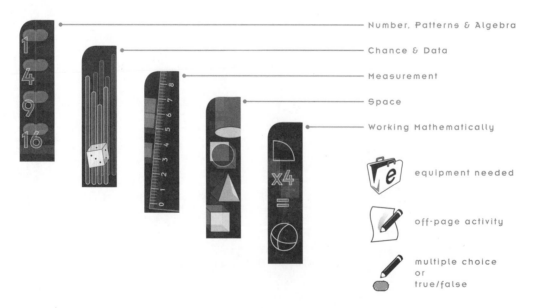

Number, Patterns & Algebra

Chance & Data

Measurement

Space

Working Mathematically

equipment needed

off-page activity

multiple choice
or
true/false

In *Enrich-e-matics 3rd Edition* explanations and worked examples are highlighted. The space for students to write answers and show their working has been maximised in this new edition. An icon has been used to show where students may need extra paper or equipment to complete the problems. Multiple choice and true/false questions use shaded bubbles similar to those used in state and national test papers.

*Enrich-e-matics 3rd Edition* is designed to meet the needs of students by:

- providing challenging problems for enrichment and extension
- reinforcing concepts and skills
- developing problem-solving strategies and extending mathematical insight, ability and logical thought
- providing opportunities to experience the joy of problem solving
- providing a ready source of challenging problems to prepare students for mathematics competitions

all of which build the foundation for excellence in mathematics.

The *Enrich-e-matics* series may be used to supplement and be integrated into the school's mathematics program.

The *Enrich-e-matics 3rd Edition Teacher's Book* is available to assist teachers implement the enrichment program in their school. It is a most valuable resource containing teaching suggestions, worked solutions and reproducible material. Most importantly it also contains highly valued screening tests that help to identify mathematical ability.

## Who can use this book?

*Enrich-e-matics 3rd Edition Book 3* may be used by:

- a group of able students working together in class
- classes in selective schools or maths extension groups
- an individual student at home.

The books have been extensively trialled, over several years, with students aged 6 to 15 in schools and at various camps for gifted and talented students. *Enrich-e-matics 3rd Edition Book 3* is aimed at 8 to 10 year olds.

To gain the maximum advantage from the series encourage students to discuss their solutions in small groups, with their teacher or with parents at home. This discussion of ideas enhances learning.

I hope that you will find *Enrich-e-matics 3rd Edition* enjoyable and challenging, and that you remain curious and motivated mathematics students.

*Anne Joshua*

# Contents

**ANSWERS**
lift-out at the back of book

# Number grids

In these grids, the sum of each row and each column has been given. What numbers must be placed in the empty boxes to make these sums? Before you start, study the worked example.

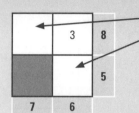

This number must be 5, as 5 + 3 = 8.

This number must be 3, as 3 + 3 = 6.

Now look at the second row:

■ + 3 = 5 and 5 + ■ = 7

so ■ = 2    Here is the solution:

**1**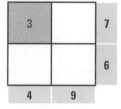

**2**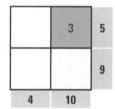

**3**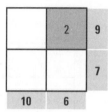

**4**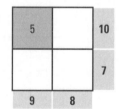

**5**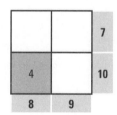

**6**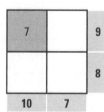

**7**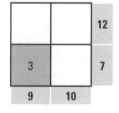

**8**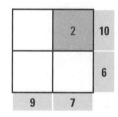

**9**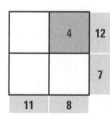

**10**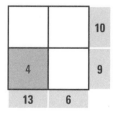

**11**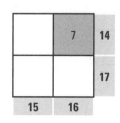

**12**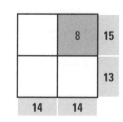

# Grid puzzles

In these grids, only the sum of each row and column is given. Using only the counting numbers, which are 1, 2, 3, 4 and so on, work out which numbers should be placed in the small empty squares. The last six questions have more than one solution. Find two different solutions.

**1**

|   |   | 4 |
|---|---|---|
|   |   | 2 |
| 4 | 2 |   |

**2**

|   |   | 4 |
|---|---|---|
|   |   | 5 |
| 2 | 7 |   |

**3**

|   |   | 5 |
|---|---|---|
|   |   | 3 |
| 6 | 2 |   |

**4**

|   |   | 10 |
|---|---|----|
|   |   | 2 |
| 6 | 6 |   |

**5**

|   |   | 3 |
|---|---|---|
|   |   | 4 |
| 2 | 5 |   |

**6**

|   |   | 2 |
|---|---|---|
|   |   | 6 |
| 3 | 5 |   |

**7**

|   |   | 4 |
|---|---|---|
|   |   | 5 |
| 4 | 5 |   |

*or*

|   |   | 4 |
|---|---|---|
|   |   | 5 |
| 4 | 5 |   |

**8**

|   |   | 6 |
|---|---|---|
|   |   | 3 |
| 4 | 5 |   |

*or*

|   |   | 6 |
|---|---|---|
|   |   | 3 |
| 4 | 5 |   |

**9**

|   |   | 8 |
|---|---|---|
|   |   | 5 |
| 7 | 6 |   |

*or*

|   |   | 8 |
|---|---|---|
|   |   | 5 |
| 7 | 6 |   |

**10**

|   |   | 5 |
|---|---|---|
|   |   | 5 |
| 5 | 5 |   |

*or*

|   |   | 5 |
|---|---|---|
|   |   | 5 |
| 5 | 5 |   |

**11**

|   |   | 8 |
|---|---|---|
|   |   | 4 |
| 6 | 6 |   |

*or*

|   |   | 8 |
|---|---|---|
|   |   | 4 |
| 6 | 6 |   |

**12**

|   |   | 7 |
|---|---|---|
|   |   | 3 |
| 5 | 5 |   |

*or*

|   |   | 7 |
|---|---|---|
|   |   | 3 |
| 5 | 5 |   |

# Missing numbers

In each set of circles, the numbers follow a certain pattern. The arrows in the first circle of each set show how the numbers should be read. What numbers are missing from the last two circles in each set? Write the rules on the small circle on the left.

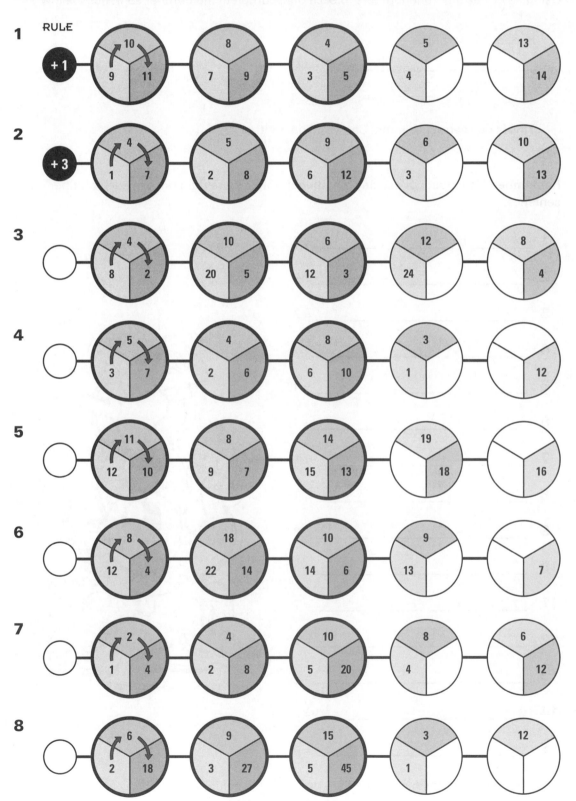

# Number sentences

In this exercise you will use only the numbers 2, 3, 4, 5 and 6.

Using any three different numbers in each one, complete the number sentences below.

Here is an example:

_____ + _____ − _____ = 6

4 + 5 − 3 = 6

This is one correct solution. Can you find another?

**Remember:** You must not use any counting number more than once in each number sentence.

1 _____ + _____ + _____ = 9

2 _____ + _____ − _____ = 9

3 _____ + _____ − _____ = 2

4 _____ + _____ − _____ = 4

5 _____ + _____ + _____ = 10

6 _____ + _____ + _____ = 11

7 _____ − _____ − _____ = 1

8 _____ − _____ − _____ = 0

9 _____ − _____ + _____ = 3

10 _____ × _____ + _____ = 10

11 _____ × _____ − _____ = 7

12 _____ × _____ − _____ = 2

13 _____ × _____ − _____ = 0

14 _____ × _____ − _____ = 3

15 _____ × _____ + _____ = 11

Some of the sentences have more than one possible solution. How many can you find?

# Number ideas

Use any combination of the symbols +, – and × to make the groups of numbers given below into true statements.

For example, if you are given the numbers 1 ☐ 4 ☐ 3 = 1, you will need the symbols × and – to make a number sentence:

1 ×̲ 4 –̲ 3 = 1

**Remember**: You must work out brackets first, and multiply (×) before you add (+) or subtract (–):

$$1 + (2 × 3) = 1 + 6$$
$$\text{(First)} \quad = 7$$

$$(1 + 2) × 3 = 3 × 3$$
$$\text{(First)} \quad = 9$$

**1** 1 ☐ 2 ☐ 3 = 0

**2** 1 ☐ 3 ☐ 2 = 1

**3** 1 ☐ 3 ☐ 2 = 2

**4** 2 ☐ 3 ☐ 1 = 4

**5** 2 ☐ 3 ☐ 1 = 5

**6** 1 ☐ 2 ☐ 3 = 6

**7** 1 ☐ 3 ☐ 4 = 7

**8** 2 ☐ 4 ☐ 6 = 0

**9** 2 ☐ 4 ☐ 6 = 2

**10** 2 ☐ 3 ☐ 5 = 1

**11** 2 ☐ 5 ☐ 6 = 4

**12** 2 ☐ 5 ☐ 1 = 9

**13** 2 ☐ 4 ☐ 3 = 5

**14** 6 ☐ 2 ☐ 4 = 8

**15** 2 ☐ 6 ☐ 4 = 4

**16** 2 ☐ 4 ☐ 5 = 3

**17** 2 ☐ 3 ☐ 1 = 7

**18** 2 ☐ 5 ☐ 2 = 12

**19** 2 ☐ 5 ☐ 2 = 8

**20** 2 ☐ 6 ☐ 5 = 7

# Numbers and symbols

In the questions below, use the numbers indicated and any combinations of the symbols +, −, ×, ÷ and brackets to make number sentences for the numbers below.

Remember the order of operations:
• brackets first;
• multiply and divide before add and subtract.

**1** Use four 2s. Here are some examples.

$$2 + 2 \times 2 - 2 \; = \; 2 + 4 - 2 \qquad\qquad (2 + 2) \times 2 - 2 \; = \; 4 \times 2 - 2$$
$$= \; 4 \qquad\qquad\qquad\qquad\qquad\qquad = \; 8 - 2$$
$$= \; 6$$

and

$$2 + 2 \times (2 - 2) \; = \; 2 + 2 \times 0$$
$$= \; 2 + 0$$
$$= \; 2$$

0 = _____      1 = _____

3 = _____      5 = _____

8 = _____      10 = _____

**2** Use three 3s. Here are some examples.

Remember the order of operations:

$$(3 - 3) \times 3 \; = \; 0 \text{ (brackets first)} \qquad\qquad 3 - 3 \div 3 \; = \; 3 - 1 \text{ (divide before subtract)}$$
$$3 + 3 \times 3 \; = \; 3 + 9 \text{ (multiply before add)} \qquad\qquad\qquad = \; 2$$
$$= \; 12$$

0 = _____      3 = _____

4 = _____      6 = _____

9 = _____      18 = _____

**3** Use four 3s. Here are some examples.

$$3 + 3 \div 3 + 3 \; = \; 3 + 1 + 3 \qquad\qquad (3 + 3) \div 3 + 3 \; = \; 6 \div 3 + 3$$
$$= \; 7 \qquad\qquad\qquad\qquad\qquad\qquad = \; 2 + 3$$
$$= \; 5$$

and

$$(3 + 3) \div (3 + 3) \; = \; 6 \div 6$$
$$= \; 1$$

0 = _____      2 = _____

3 = _____      6 = _____

9 = _____      10 = _____

# Square puzzles

In this exercise, you will use only the numbers 1, 2, 3, 4 and 5.

Using the sums of the rows and columns given for these divided squares, work out the values of the letters A, B, C and D and write your solutions in the blank grids provided. **Note that the letters each have a different value and are different for each question.**

You will have to use the method of 'guess and check' for questions 7 to 10.

**1**

A = _____

B = _____

C = _____

**2**

A = _____

B = _____

C = _____

**3**

A = _____

B = _____

C = _____

**4**

A = _____

B = _____

C = _____

**5**

 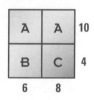

A = _____

B = _____

C = _____

**6**

A = _____

B = _____

C = _____

**7**

A = _____

B = _____

C = _____

D = _____

**8**

A = _____

B = _____

C = _____

D = _____

**9**

A = _____

B = _____

C = _____

D = _____

**10**

A = _____

B = _____

C = _____

D = _____

# Find my rule

In each question, there is a set of boxes. Every box follows the same rule. Find the rule, write it down, and then use it to work out which numbers are missing from the last box.

The rule for question 1 is 'Subtract 3 from the first number and double the answer', written − 3, × 2.

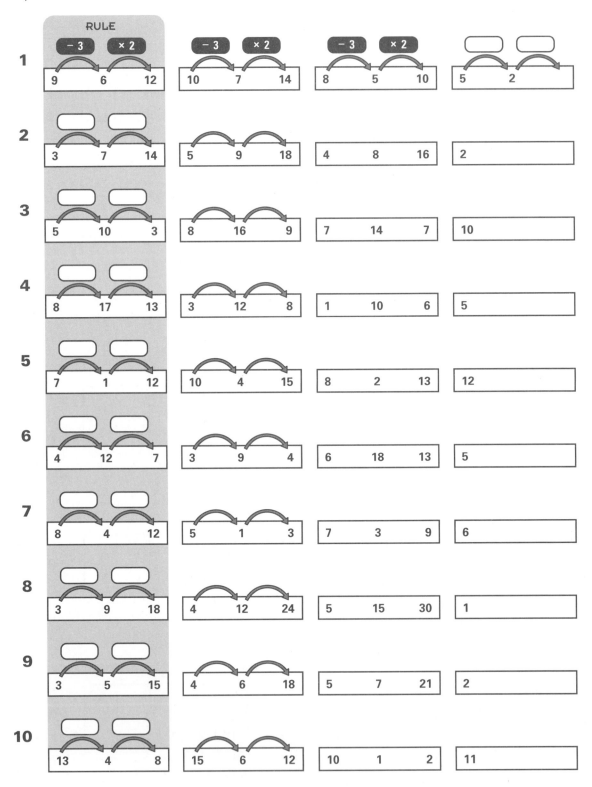

# What's the rule?

In each question, there is a set of boxes. Every box follows the same rule. Find the rule, write it down and then use it to work out which numbers are missing from the last box.

The rule for question 1 is 'Multiply the first number by 3, then subtract 4', written × 3, – 4.

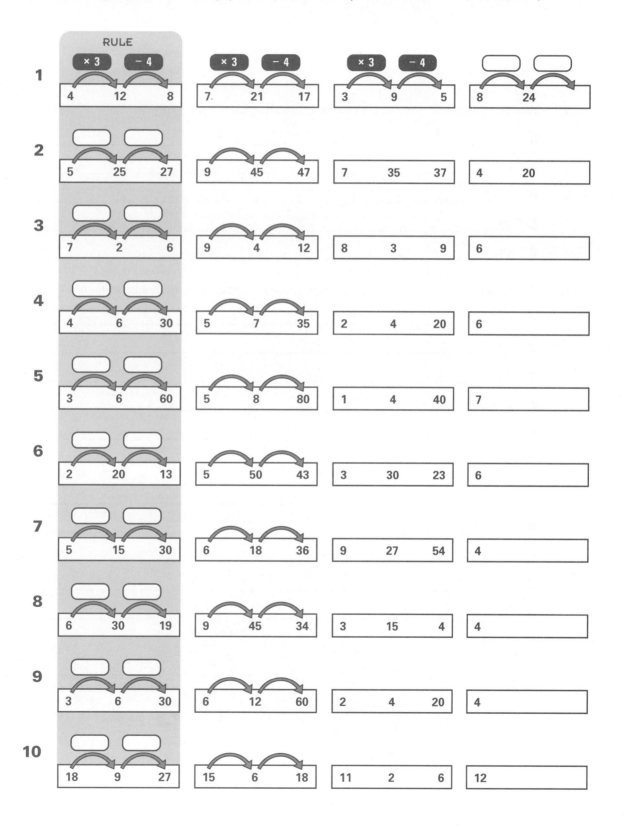

# Which two numbers?

1, 2, 3, 4, ... are counting numbers.

**Question:** Which two counting numbers can be added to give a sum of 8?

**Answer:** $1 + 7 = 8$,  $2 + 6 = 8$,  $3 + 5 = 8$,  $4 + 4 = 8$ are all the possible solutions.

There are many solutions to the questions below. Can you list them all?
Remember to work systematically.

**1** Which two counting numbers can be added to give the sum of:

   **a** 5?    $\underline{\hspace{1cm}1\hspace{1cm}} + \underline{\hspace{1cm}4\hspace{1cm}} = 5,$   _____

   **b** 6? _____

   **c** 10? _____

   **d** 12? _____

   **e** 15? _____

**2** Which two counting numbers can be multiplied together to give a product of:

   **a** 6? _____

   **b** 12? _____

   **c** 16? _____

   **d** 20? _____

   **e** 24? _____

**3** Which two counting numbers have a difference of:

   **a** 3? _____

   **b** 5? _____

   **c** 6? _____

   **d** 10? _____

   **e** 17? _____

# Find two numbers

The product of two numbers is the result you get when you multiply one by the other. The product of 3 and 4 is 12.

Look at this table.

| Numbers whose sum is 10 | 1, 9 | 2, 8 | 3, 7 | 4, 6 | 5, 5 |
|---|---|---|---|---|---|
| The product of these numbers: | 9 | 16 | 21 | 24 | 25 |

To find the answers to the following questions you may need to draw up a table like this and list all the possibilities.

Find the two numbers I am thinking of if:

**1** the sum of the numbers is 7 and their product is 10. _____

**2** the sum of the numbers is 10 and their product is 16. _____

**3** the sum of the numbers is 10 and their product is 21. _____

**4** the sum of the numbers is 10 and their product is 9. _____

**5** the sum of the numbers is 9 and their product is 14. _____

**6** the sum of the numbers is 9 and their product is 8. _____

**7** the sum of the numbers is 7 and their difference is 3. _____

**8** the sum of the numbers is 8 and their difference is 6. _____

**9** the sum of the numbers is 8 and their difference is 2. _____

**10** the sum of the numbers is 11 and their difference is 1. _____

**11** the sum of the numbers is 12 and their difference is 4. _____

**12** the sum of the numbers is 12 and their difference is 8. _____

**13** the sum of two numbers is 5, and one is 1 more than the other. _____

**14** the sum of two numbers is 8, and one is 2 more than the other. _____

**15** the sum of two numbers is 8, and one is 4 more than the other. _____

**16** the sum of two numbers is 12, and one is 2 more than the other. _____

**17** the sum of two numbers is 11, and one is 1 more than the other. _____

**18** the sum of two numbers is 15, and one is 1 more than the other. _____

**19** the sum of two numbers is 15, and one is 3 more than the other. _____

**20** the sum of two numbers is 9, and one is double the other. _____

**21** the sum of two numbers is 18, and one is double the other. _____

**22** the sum of two numbers is 30, and one is double the other. _____

**23** the sum of two numbers is 21, and one is double the other. _____

**24** the sum of two numbers is 27, and one is double the other. _____

# Number puzzles

In these exercises, the numbers to be used must each appear only *once* in a diagram.

**1** Place the numbers 1 to 5 in the circles so that the sum of the numbers in each line is:

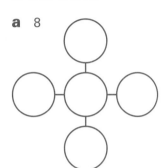 **a** 8

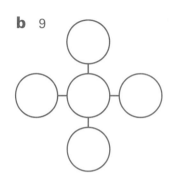 **b** 9

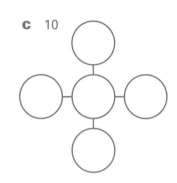 **c** 10

**2** Place the numbers 2 to 6 in the empty circles so that the sum of the numbers along the sides of the squares is:

**a** 12     **b** 13     **c** 14     **d** 15

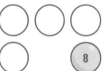 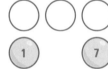  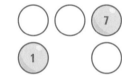

**3** Place the numbers 1 to 7 in the empty boxes so that each horizontal and vertical line forms a true statement.

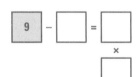

**4** Arrange the numbers 3 to 8 in these squares so that each vertical and horizontal set forms a true statement.

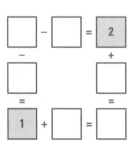

Number, Patterns & Algebra

# Magic squares

A square is said to be 'magic' when the numbers in all horizontal, vertical and diagonal lines have the same sum.

| 10 | 3 | 8 |
|----|----|----|
| 5 | 7 | 9 |
| 6 | 11 | 4 |

This is an example of a magic square.

Check each horizontal, vertical and diagonal line to see that the magic sum is 21.

In these exercises, each magic square uses the given numbers only *once*.

**1** If the numbers used are 1 to 9, and the sum of each line is 15 (the magic sum is 15), what are the missing numbers? **Remember:** No digit can be repeated.

**a**

| 8 |  | 6 |
|----|----|----|
|  |  |  |
| 4 | 9 |  |

**b**

|  | 7 | 2 |
|----|----|----|
|  |  |  |
| 8 | 3 |  |

**c**

| 4 |  |  |
|----|----|----|
|  | 5 |  |
| 2 |  | 6 |

**2** In these magic squares, the numbers 0 to 8 are used. Find the missing numbers that will make a magic sum of 12.

**a**

|  |  | 5 |
|----|----|----|
| 2 |  |  |
|  | 8 | 1 |

**b**

|  |  | 3 |
|----|----|----|
|  | 4 |  |
| 5 | 0 |  |

**c**

| 3 |  | 7 |
|----|----|----|
|  |  |  |
|  |  | 6 |

**3** These squares use the numbers 1 to 10. Which numbers will be needed to make a magic sum of 18?

**a**

| 9 | 2 |  |
|----|----|----|
|  | 6 |  |
|  |  | 3 |

**b**

| 7 |  | 3 |
|----|----|----|
|  |  | 10 |
|  |  |  |

**c**

| 5 | 4 |  |
|----|----|----|
|  |  |  |
|  | 8 |  |

# Patterns and sequences

A sequence is a group of numbers that follows a pattern.

In each group below, find the pattern, then by working out the differences between the terms, write down the next three numbers in the sequence.

**1**  2, 4, 6, 8, _____ , _____ , _____

**2**  3, 5, 7, 9, _____ , _____ , _____

**3**  7, 11, 15, 19, _____ , _____ , _____

**4**  2, 9, 16, 23, _____ , _____ , _____

**5**  10, 20, 30, 40, _____ , _____ , _____

**6**  5, 10, 15, 20, _____ , _____ , _____

**7**  11, 14, 17, 20, _____ , _____ , _____

**8**  5, 15, 25, 35, _____ , _____ , _____

**9**  1, 9, 17, 25, _____ , _____ , _____

**10**  21, 23, 25, 27, _____ , _____ , _____

**11**  30, 25, 20, 15, _____ , _____ , _____

**12**  50, 48, 46, 44, _____ , _____ , _____

**13**  90, 80, 70, 60, _____ , _____ , _____

**14**  23, 20, 17, 14, _____ , _____ , _____

**15**  42, 38, 34, 30, _____ , _____ , _____

**16**  48, 43, 38, 33, _____ , _____ , _____

**17**  4, 8, 12, 16, _____ , _____ , _____

**18**  7, 14, 21, 28, _____ , _____ , _____

**19**  18, 16, 14, 12, _____ , _____ , _____

**20**  12, 23, 34, 45, _____ , _____ , _____

**21**  3, 6, 9, 12, _____ , _____ , _____

**22**  6, 12, 18, 24, _____ , _____ , _____

**23**  1, 10, 19, 28, _____ , _____ , _____

**24**  89, 80, 71, 62, _____ , _____ , _____

**25**  63, 56, 49, 42, _____ , _____ , _____

**26**  53, 47, 41, 35, _____ , _____ , _____

**27**  38, 50, 62, 74, _____ , _____ , _____

**28**  120, 105, 90, 75, _____ , _____ , _____

**29**  7, 20, 33, 46, _____ , _____ , _____

**30**  100, 89, 78, 67, _____ , _____ , _____

_____ , _____ , _____ , _____ , _____ ,

# Missing numbers

Find the missing number in each sequence. Work out the differences between the terms. Some sequences have 2 patterns.

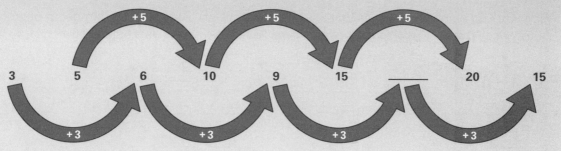

so the missing number is 12.

OR

so the missing number is 16.

**1**  3, 6, _____ , 12, 15, 18, 21

**2**  24, 21, _____ , 15, 12, 9, 6

**3**  65, 60, 55, _____ , 45, 40, 35

**4**  97, 93, _____ , 85, 81, 77, 73

**5**  21, 25, 29, _____ , 37, 41, 45

**6**  34, 45, 56, _____ , 78, 89

**7**  1, 2, 4, 7, 11, _____ , 22, 29

**8**  30, 29, 27, 24, 20, _____ , 9, 2

**9**  65, 67, 70, _____ , 79, 85, 92

**10**  97, 96, 94, _____ , 87, 82, 76

**11**  1, 3, 6, 10, _____ , 21, 28, 36

**12**  6, 9, 8, 11, 10, 13, _____ , 15, 14

**13**  2, 10, 4, 20, 6, _____ , 8, 40, 10

**14**  1, 5, 3, 10, 5, 15, _____ , 20, 9

**15**  3, 10, 8, 12, _____ , 14, 18, 16, 23

**16**  3, 9, 7, 13, 11, 17, 15, _____ , 19

**17**  97, 95, 87, 90, _____ , 85, 67, 80, 57

**18**  28, _____ , 29, 35, 30, 34, 31, 33, 32

**19**  39, 7, 34, 10, _____ , 13, 24, 16, 19

**20**  73, 1, 64, 5, 55, 9, _____ , 13, 37

# Find three numbers

In each question, I am thinking of three different numbers: $\square$ , $\triangle$ and $\bigcirc$ .
Using the clues given, find my three numbers.

First work on number sentences that use one number only. Then use this number in other number sentences to work out other numbers. 'Guess and check' is a helpful strategy.

**1**  $\triangle + \triangle = 6$

$\triangle + \bigcirc = \square$

$\square + \bigcirc = 7$

$\square + \square = 10$

**2**  $\triangle + \triangle = 8$

$\triangle + \triangle + \triangle = \bigcirc + \bigcirc$

$\square + \square = \bigcirc$

**3**  $\triangle + \triangle = 14$

$\triangle - \bigcirc = 2$

$\triangle - \square = 4$

$\bigcirc + \triangle + \square = 15$

**4**  $\square + \square = 12$

$\triangle - \square = \bigcirc$

$\bigcirc + \bigcirc + \bigcirc = \square$

$\triangle + \bigcirc = 10$

**5**  $\triangle + \triangle + \triangle = 12$

$\triangle - \square = 1$

$\square + \square + \square = \bigcirc$

$\bigcirc + \triangle = 13$

**6**  $\triangle + \square = 8$

$\square + \bigcirc = 16$

$\triangle + \bigcirc = 12$

$\triangle + \triangle + \triangle + \triangle = 8$

**7**  $\triangle + \triangle = 12$

$\triangle + \bigcirc = \square$

$\triangle - \bigcirc = 1$

$\bigcirc + \bigcirc + \bigcirc = 15$

**8**  $\triangle + \triangle = 18$

$\triangle - \square = 5$

$\bigcirc - \triangle = 3$

$\bigcirc - \square = 8$

**9**  $\bigcirc + \bigcirc + \bigcirc = 9$

$\square + \bigcirc = 10$

$\triangle - \square = 6$

$\triangle - \bigcirc = 10$

**10**  $\square + \square + \square = 18$

$\triangle + \triangle = 22$

$\triangle - \square = 5$

$\bigcirc - \square = 2$

# Which three numbers?

In each question, I am thinking of three different numbers: $\square$, $\triangle$ and $\bigcirc$.
Using the clues given, find my three numbers.

'Guess and check' is a helpful strategy.

**1**
$\triangle + \triangle = 12$
$\triangle + \bigcirc = 10$
$\bigcirc + \square = 11$

**2**
$\bigcirc + \bigcirc + \bigcirc = 15$
$\square - \bigcirc = 4$
$\triangle - \square = 1$

**3**
$\triangle + \triangle + \triangle = 9$
$\square - \triangle = 9$
$\bigcirc - \square = 9$

**4**
$\square + \bigcirc = 6$
$\square - \bigcirc = 2$
$\bigcirc + \bigcirc = \square$
$\triangle + \bigcirc = 3$

**5**
$\bigcirc + \triangle = 12$
$\bigcirc - \triangle = 6$
$\triangle + \triangle + \triangle = \bigcirc$
$\square + \bigcirc = 10$

**6**
$\square + \square = \triangle$
$\square + \triangle = 12$
$\bigcirc + \bigcirc = \square$
$\bigcirc + \triangle = 10$

**7**
$\bigcirc + \bigcirc + \bigcirc = \square + \square$
$\bigcirc + \square = 5$
$\triangle - \square = 5$

**8**
$\triangle + \bigcirc = 8$
$\triangle - \bigcirc = 2$
$\bigcirc + \bigcirc = \square$
$\square - \triangle = 1$

**9**
$\bigcirc + \square = 7$
$\bigcirc + \bigcirc + \bigcirc = \square + \square + \square + \square$
$\bigcirc + \bigcirc = \triangle$
$\triangle - \square = 5$

**10**
$\triangle + \triangle = \bigcirc + 1$
$\bigcirc - \triangle = 4$
$\bigcirc + \triangle = 14$
$\square + \square + \square = \bigcirc$
$\bigcirc - \square = 6$

# Arrange the numbers

**1** Arrange the numbers from 1 to 6 in the circles so that the sum of the digits along each side is:

**a** 9

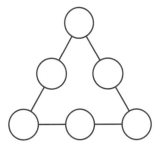

**b** 10

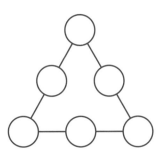

**c** 11

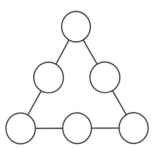

**d** 12

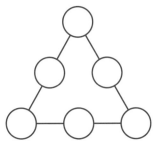

**2** Arrange the numbers 4, 5, 6, 7, 8 and 9 in the empty circles so that the digits along each side add up to 17.

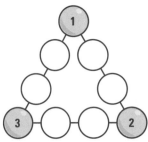

**3** Arrange the numbers from 1 to 9 in the circles of each figure so that the sum along each line is the number given above the figure.

**a** 12

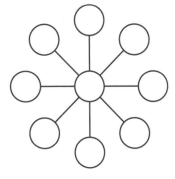

**b** 15

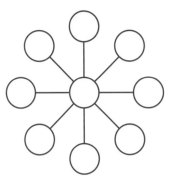

**c** 18

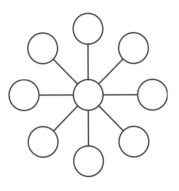

**Hint:** Try 1 in the centre.

Number, Patterns & Algebra

# What's the value?

Each shape used in these sentences stands for one of the numbers from 0 to 9.
Can you find the value of each one?

$\bigcirc \times \bigcirc = \bigcirc$

$\bigcirc + \bigcirc = \square$

$\square \times \square = \square + \square = \triangle$

$\square + \triangleright = \square$

$\bigcirc + \bigcirc + \bigcirc = \bigcirc$

$\bigcirc \times \square = \text{◗}$

$\square + \bigcirc = \diagup\!\!\!\diagdown$

$\diagup\!\!\!\diagdown + \bigcirc = \text{◗}$

$\diagup\!\!\!\diagdown + \square = \bigcirc$

$\bigcirc + \square = \rectangle$

$\bigcirc + \bigcirc + \bigcirc = \rectangle$

$\rectangle - \bigcirc = \triangle$

$\triangle \div \square = \triangleright$

# What's the question?

**1** If you have to add three numbers to get an answer of 5, possible questions are:

$1 + 1 + 3 =$   or   $1 + 2 + 2 =$

If you have to use five different numbers to get an answer of 5 and you can add, subtract, multiply or divide to do it, possible questions are:

$3 \times 4 - 2 + 1 - 6 =$   or   $15 \div 5 + 4 + 8 - 10 =$   or   $1 + 2 + 3 + 4 - 5 =$

Write down some possible questions to which the answer is 8, where you have to:

**a** add two numbers; _____

**b** add four numbers; _____

**c** find the difference of two numbers; _____

**d** use five numbers and any mathematical operation (+, −, × or ÷);

_____

**e** use division; _____

**f** use fractions and multiplication. _____

**2** Place digits in these squares so that the sums of the numbers are those given.

**a**     **b**    **c**

How many solutions can you find for **a**, **b** and **c**?

**3** Place the digits 1, 2, 3 and 4 in these squares so that the sum of the numbers is 55. Now try to do this another way. How many solutions can you find? Do not repeat digits.

**4** Place the digits 3, 4, 5 and 6 in these squares so that the sum of the numbers is 99. How many solutions can you find? Do not repeat digits.

# Past numbers

**1** Babylonian cuneiform (wedge writing) numerals consisted of two symbols only:

⋎  for 1     12 was written like this: ⟨⋎⋎

⟨  for 10     24 was written like this: ⟨⟨⋎⋎⋎⋎

31 was written like this: ⟨⟨⟨⋎

**a** What do the following symbols represent in our number system?

**i** ⋎⋎⋎ _____

**ii** ⟨⟨ _____

**iii** ⟨⋎ _____

**iv** ⟨⟨⟨⋎⋎⋎ _____

**v** ⟨⋎⋎⋎⋎⋎⋎ _____

**b** Write the following numbers in Babylonian cuneiform script.

**i** 4 _____

**ii** 13 _____

**iii** 26 _____

**iv** 30 _____

**v** 45 _____

**2** Mayan people used dots and strokes to represent numbers up to twenty.

This was 3: •••

This was 18: ••• (5 + 5 + 5 + 3)

This was 5: —

This was 9: •••• (5 + 4)

**a** What do the following symbols represent in our number system?

**i** •••• _____

**ii** • _____

**iii** •• _____

**iv** ≡ _____

**v** •••• _____

**b** Write the following numbers as Mayan numerals.

**i** 2 _____

**ii** 7 _____

**iii** 9 _____

**iv** 11 _____

**v** 16 _____

# Continue the pattern

In each exercise, continue the pattern for two more lines; check your answers on a calculator. Don't forget to treat brackets first.

**1**
$1 \times 9 = 10 - 1$
$2 \times 9 = 20 - 2$
$3 \times 9 = 30 - 3$
$4 \times 9 = 40 - 4$

_____

_____

**2**
$1 \times 8 = 10 - 2$
$2 \times 8 = 20 - 4$
$3 \times 8 = 30 - 6$
$4 \times 8 = 40 - 8$

_____

_____

**3**
$1 + 2 + 1 = 4 = 2 \times 2$
$1 + 2 + 3 + 2 + 1 = 9 = 3 \times 3$
$1 + 2 + 3 + 4 + 3 + 2 + 1 = 16 = 4 \times 4$
$1 + 2 + 3 + 4 + 5 + 4 + 3 + 2 + 1 = 25 = 5 \times 5$

_____

_____

**4**
$1 = 2 - 1 \times 1$
$1 + 2 = 3 + 4 - 2 \times 2$
$1 + 2 + 3 = 4 + 5 + 6 - 3 \times 3$
$1 + 2 + 3 + 4 = 5 + 6 + 7 + 8 - 4 \times 4$

_____

_____

**5**
$1 + 2 = 3$
$4 + 5 + 6 = 7 + 8$
$9 + 10 + 11 + 12 = 13 + 14 + 15$

_____

_____

**6**
$(2 - 1) \times (2 + 1) = 3 = 2 + 1$
$(3 - 2) \times (3 + 2) = 5 = 3 + 2$
$(4 - 3) \times (4 + 3) = 7 = 4 + 3$

_____

_____

**7**
$(2 - 1) \times (2 + 1) = 3$
$(3 - 1) \times (3 + 1) = 8$
$(4 - 1) \times (4 + 1) = 15$

_____

_____

**8**
$(2 - 0) \times (2 + 0) = 2 \times 2$
$(3 - 1) \times (3 + 1) = 2 \times 4$
$(4 - 2) \times (4 + 2) = 2 \times 6$

_____

_____

# Shapes and values

In each of these figures, every shape has a different value and the sums of the rows and columns are given. Find the value of each shape. Enter the values in the grids as you find them.

In question **1**, first find the value of ◯ by looking at the first column sum:

◯ + ◯ + ◯ = 12, so ◯ = 4. Fill in this value.

Then find the value of △ by looking at the first row sum:

4 + △ + 4 = 13, so △ = 5.

Continue in this way to find the value of all the other shapes.

**1**

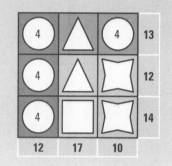

**2**

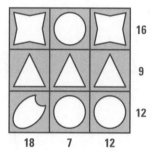

**3**

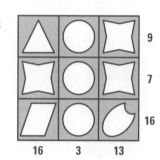

**4**

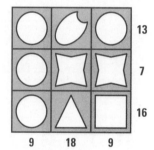

**5**

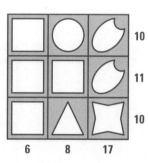

**6**

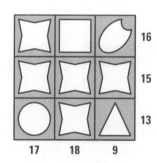

**7**

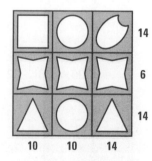

**8**

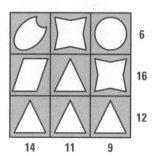

**9**

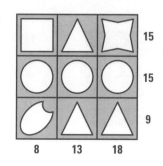

**10**

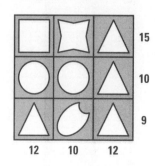

# Related rows

In each set of two rows, there is a relationship between the numbers in the first row and those in the second row below it. For example, in set 1 each number in the second row is 5 more than the one above it.

Work out the rule for each set, and then find the missing number.

**1**

| 13 | 7 | 9 | 11 | 6 | Rule |
|----|----|----|----|----|------|
| 18 | 12 | 14 | 16 |  | + 5 |

**2**

| 4 | 7 | 3 | 5 | 2 | Rule |
|----|----|----|----|----|------|
| 8 | 14 | 6 | 10 |  |  |

**3**

| 14 | 27 | 13 | 15 | 12 | Rule |
|----|----|----|----|----|------|
| 6 | 19 | 5 | 7 |  |  |

**4**

| 6 | 4 | 7 | 9 | 5 | Rule |
|----|----|----|----|----|------|
| 60 | 40 | 70 | 90 |  |  |

**5**

| 4 | 7 | 3 | 5 | 2 | Rule |
|----|----|----|----|----|------|
| 16 | 28 | 12 | 20 |  |  |

**6**

| 1 | 8 | 4 | 7 | 9 | Rule |
|----|----|----|----|----|------|
| 7 | 14 | 10 | 13 |  |  |

**7**

| 7 | 9 | 4 | 5 | 1 | Rule |
|----|----|----|----|----|------|
| 35 | 45 | 20 | 25 |  |  |

**8**

| 7 | 9 | 11 | 5 | 6 | Rule |
|----|----|----|----|----|------|
| 14 | 18 | 22 | 10 |  |  |

**9**

| 7 | 9 | 11 | 5 | 6 | Rule |
|----|----|----|----|----|------|
| 15 | 19 | 23 | 11 |  |  |

**10**

| 4 | 7 | 3 | 5 | 2 | Rule |
|----|----|----|----|----|------|
| 7 | 13 | 5 | 9 |  |  |

**11**

| 4 | 8 | 7 | 6 | 5 | Rule |
|----|----|----|----|----|------|
| 39 | 79 | 69 | 59 |  |  |

**12**

| 8 | 4 | 3 | 10 | 2 | Rule |
|----|----|----|----|----|------|
| 39 | 19 | 14 | 49 |  |  |

**13**

| 7 | 9 | 8 | 2 | 6 | Rule |
|----|----|----|----|----|------|
| 28 | 36 | 32 | 8 |  |  |

**14**

| 7 | 9 | 8 | 2 | 6 | Rule |
|----|----|----|----|----|------|
| 29 | 37 | 33 | 9 |  |  |

**15**

| 4 | 7 | 3 | 5 | 2 | Rule |
|----|----|----|----|----|------|
| 13 | 22 | 10 | 16 |  |  |

**16**

| 4 | 8 | 7 | 5 | 3 | Rule |
|----|----|----|----|----|------|
| 21 | 41 | 36 | 26 |  |  |

**17**

| 6 | 5 | 2 | 3 | 4 | Rule |
|----|----|----|----|----|------|
| 36 | 25 | 4 | 9 |  |  |

**18**

| 6 | 5 | 2 | 3 | 4 | Rule |
|----|----|----|----|----|------|
| 35 | 24 | 3 | 8 |  |  |

**19**

| 14 | 27 | 13 | 9 | 8 | Rule |
|----|----|----|----|----|------|
| 9 | 22 | 8 | 4 |  |  |

**20**

| 1 | 2 | 3 | 4 | 5 | Rule |
|----|----|----|----|----|------|
| 2 | 5 | 10 | 17 |  |  |

# Differences

In this exercise, you start with four numbers at the corners of the large square.

In the middle of each side, you write down the difference between the two corner numbers.

Then in the middle of the smaller square, you write down the difference between the two corner numbers.

This is repeated until you have zero on all the corners.

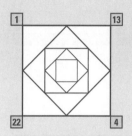 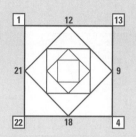 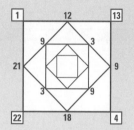 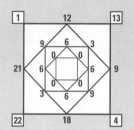

Complete the differences for the squares below.

**1**
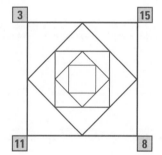

**2**
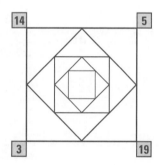

**3**
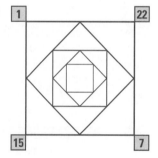

**4**
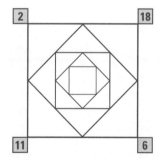

**5**
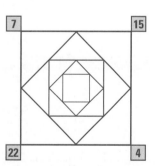

**6**
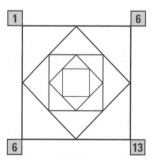

**7**
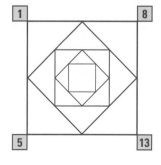

**8**
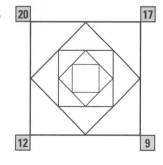

**9**
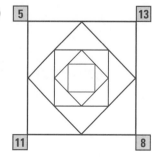

# Number line

Here is part of a number line. Write in the number shown by the arrow.

**1**

10        20

**2**

100        200

**3**

1000        2000

**4**
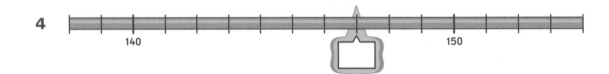

140        150

**5**

220        230

**6**

1100        1200

**7**

450        470

**8**

10        40

Number, Patterns & Algebra

# Find the value

There is a short cut to work out the sum

$$55 - 45 + 35 - 25 + 15 - 5$$

By grouping the numbers in pairs

$$(55 - 45) + (35 - 25) + (15 - 5)$$
$$= 10 + 10 + 10$$
$$= 30.$$

Find the value of each of the following by looking for a short cut first.

**1**  $10 - 9 + 8 - 7 + 6 - 5 + 4 - 3 + 2 - 1 =$ _____

**2**  $100 - 90 + 80 - 70 + 60 - 50 + 40 - 30 + 20 - 10 =$ _____

**3**  $120 - 100 + 80 - 60 + 40 - 20 =$ _____

**4**  $40 - 35 + 30 - 25 + 20 - 15 + 10 - 5 =$ _____

**5**  $18 - 15 + 12 - 9 + 6 - 3 =$ _____

**6**  $24 - 20 + 16 - 12 + 8 - 4 =$ _____

**7**  $100 - 95 + 90 - 85 + 80 - 75 + 70 - 65 + 60 - 55 =$ _____

**8**  $600 - 500 + 400 - 300 + 200 - 100 =$ _____

**9**  $150 - 125 + 100 - 75 + 50 - 25 =$ _____

**10**  $300 - 270 + 240 - 210 + 180 - 150 + 120 - 90 + 60 - 30 =$ _____

# Counting-frame arithmetic

A counting frame uses place value to show numbers. Starting from the right-hand side, the 2 beads on the first wire represent 2 ones. The 1 bead on the next wire represents 1 ten. The 3 beads on the third wire represent 3 hundreds. So the number on the counting frame is 312.

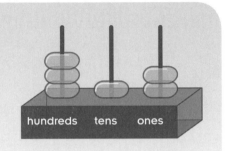

**1** Imagine that you start with a 3-spike counting frame and 2 beads. Using *both* beads each time, write down the number you will have on the counting frame if you make:

    **a** the smallest number possible  _____

    **b** the largest number possible  _____

    **c** the largest even number  _____

    **d** the largest odd number  _____

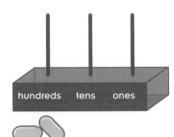

**2** This time you have 3 beads and the counting frame. Using *all 3* beads each time, write down the number you get when you make:

    **a** the smallest 2-digit number possible  _____

    **b** the smallest even number  _____

    **c** the smallest odd number  _____

    **d** the largest number possible  _____

    **e** the largest 2-digit number possible  _____

    **f** the largest even number  _____

    **g** the largest odd number  _____

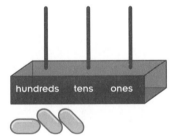

**3** Now you have 4 beads and a 3-spike counting frame. Draw and write down *all* the numbers you can make if you use all four beads each time. There are 15 solutions (**a–o**). Start with the smallest number 4, then move one bead to make a larger number. Remember to work systematically.

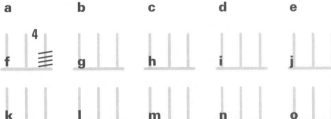

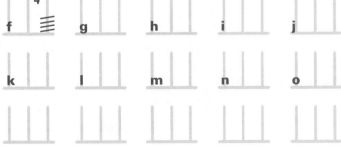

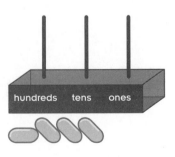

Number, Patterns & Algebra

# Shading parts

**1** One half of each of these shapes has been shaded.

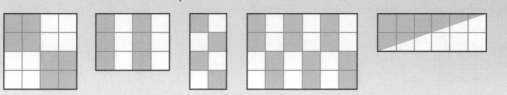

Can you shade half of each of these shapes in three different ways? If you can find more solutions, draw them on squared paper.

**a** 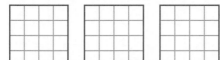  **b**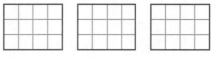

**c** 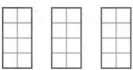  **d**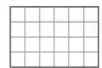

**e**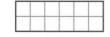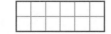

**2** One-quarter of each of these shapes has been shaded.

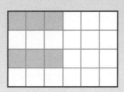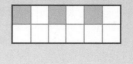

Can you shade one-quarter of each of these shapes in two different ways?

**a** 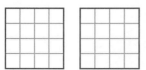  **b** 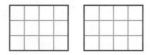  **c**

**d** 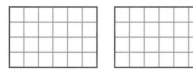  **e**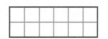

# What fraction's shaded ?

Write down the fraction shaded in each diagram and, on the next diagram, shade another possible way of illustrating the same fraction shaded.

**1** 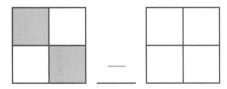 ____

**2** 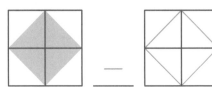 ____

**3** 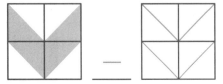 ____

**4** 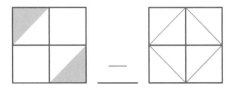 ____

**5** 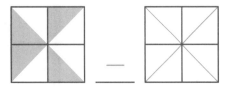 ____

**6** 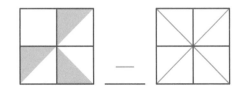 ____

**7** 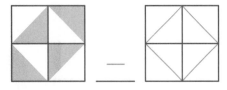 ____

**8**  ____

**9**  ____

**10**  ____

# How old?

**1** Douglas is 5 years younger than Helen.
Helen is 10. How old will Douglas be 3 years from now? _____

**2** Nadia is 4 years older than Ivan.
Ivan is 15. How old will Nadia be in 5 years from now? _____

**3** Andrew is 4 years older than his younger sister, Tina, and he is 5 years younger than his older brother, Jeremy. The sum of the three children's ages is 34.
How old is Andrew? _____

**Hint:** Use a table like this one and the guess-and-check method to work out this problem. The first guess has been made for you.

| Andrew | Tina | Jeremy | Sum of ages | |
|--------|------|--------|-------------|--------|
| 10 | 6 | 15 | 31 | *Too low* |
| | | | | |

**4** Mrs Smart has three children: Brenda, Jacob and Tammy. Brenda is twice as old as Jacob. Tammy is 6 years older than Jacob. When Brenda was born, Tammy was 2. The sum of the ages of the three children is 22. How old are the children?

| Brenda | Jacob | Tammy | Sum of ages |
|--------|-------|-------|-------------|
| | | | |

**5** Mr and Mrs Wong have three children: a 9-year-old boy and twin girls.
If the sum of the ages of the three children is 21, how old are the twins? _____

**6** Mrs Chong has four children: an 8-year-old girl and triplet boys. If the sum of the ages of the four children is 23, how old are the triplets?

| Daughter | Each triplet | Total age |
|----------|--------------|-----------|
| 8 | | 23 |

**7** Lydia, Yvonne, Greg and Barbara are cousins.
Greg is 10 years older than Barbara.
Yvonne is twice as old as Barbara.
Barbara is 4 years old.
Greg is twice as old as Lydia.
How old are the four cousins?

| Lydia | Yvonne | Greg | Barbara |
|-------|--------|------|---------|
| | | | |

# Coins

If I have two 20 cent coins and one 10 cent coin, I can pay for something costing 10c, 20c, 30c, 40c or 50c with these coins.

Note that  30c = 20c + 10c

40c = 20c + 20c

50c = 20c + 20c + 10c

If I have three 10 cent coins and one 5 cent coin, I can pay for something costing 5c, 10c, 15c, 20c, 25c, 30c or 35c with these coins.

List all the possible amounts that I can pay with the following coins:

**1** three 20c coins and one 5c coin

_____

**2** two 20c coins, one 10c coin and one 5c coin

_____

**3** one 50c coin and two 20c coins

_____

**4** one $1 coin, two 50c coins and one 10c coin

_____

**5** one $1 coin, one 50c coin and two 10c coins

_____

Number, Patterns & Algebra

# Money problems

**1**   How many 20 cent coins are worth $1?   _____

**2**   How many 50 cent coins are worth $4?   _____

**3**   You have a large collection of 5 cent, 10 cent and 20 cent coins.
In how many different ways can you make 40 cents?   _____
Work systematically to complete the following table.

| 20c | 10c | 5c |
|-----|-----|-----|
| 2 | – | – |
| 1 | 2 | – |
|  |  |  |
|  |  |  |
|  |  |  |
|  |  |  |
|  |  |  |
|  |  |  |
|  |  |  |

**4**   If 2 ice creams cost $1.50,
what is the cost of:

   **a**   4 ice creams?   _____

   **b**   1 ice cream?   _____

   **c**   3 ice creams?   _____

**5**   If 3 pencils cost $1.20,
what is the cost of:

   **a**   6 pencils?   _____

   **b**   9 pencils?   _____

   **c**   1 pencil?   _____

**6**   Sheila had $6 in her purse.
She spent half of it on lunch, and then half of what she had
left on a magazine. How much money does Sheila have now?   _____

**7**   Melanie spent half her pocket money, then put half of the remaining amount
in the bank. She then had $2 left.
How much pocket money does Melanie get?   _____

**8**   Lollies cost 15c each and biscuits cost 22c each.

   **a**   How many lollies could I buy with $1?   _____

      How much change would I get?   _____

   **b**   How many biscuits could I buy with $1?   _____

      How much change would I get?   _____

# How much money?

**1**  **a** How many 20c coins are needed to make $3.60? _____

    **b** How many 50c coins are needed to make $3.50? _____

    **c** How many 20c coins are needed to make $5.40? _____

**2** Gabrielle has these coins in her purse:

    **a** If she wants to buy a sandwich for $2 how much extra does she need? _____

    **b** If she buys a drink for $1.10 how much does she have left? _____

**3** Benjamin is given $3 pocket money each week. Below is a record of the money he spent over 4 weeks. How much does he save these 4 weeks? _____

|  | Week 1 | Week 2 | Week 3 | Week 4 | Total |
|---|---|---|---|---|---|
| **Spent** | $1.80 | 70c | $2.10 | $1.50 | |
| **Saved** | | | | | |

**4** I have the following coins:

    **a** Write down two different ways I can pay for a drink costing 90c.

    _____ , _____

    **b** Write down three different ways I can pay for an ice-block costing $1.60

    _____ , _____

    _____

**5** Sarah buys four 50 cent stamps and seven 20 cent stamps. How much change does she get from $5? _____

Number, Patterns & Algebra

# Missing shapes

In each exercise below, the space shows where two shapes must be drawn in order to complete the pattern. Draw the missing shapes.

**1** □ ○ □ ○ ○ □ ○ □ ○ ____ ○ □ ○ ○ □ ○

**2** ⬭ ◻ ◻ ⬭ ◻ ◻ ⬭ ◻ ◻ _____

**3** ⬤ ○ ◎ ⬤ ○ ◎ ⬤ ____ ⬤ ○ ◎ ⬤ ○

**4** ⬮ □ ○ ○ ○ ⬮ ____ ○ ○ ⬮ □ ○ ○ ○ ⬮ □ ○ ○ ○

**5** ○ ▲ ○ ○ ◇ ○ ▲ _____ ◇ ○ ▲ ○ ○ ◇

**6** ▱ ◆ □ ◆ ▱ ◆ ____ ▱ ◆ □ ◆ ▱ ◆ □ ◆

**7** ● △ ● ● □ ● △ ● ● ____ △ ● ● □ ● △

**8** △ ▯ △ △ △ ▯ △ ▯ △ △ ____ △ ▯ △ △

**9** ● // ● ● ● \ ● // ● ● ___ ● // ● ● ● \ ● // ● ● ● \

**10** □ □ | □ ● □ □ | ____ □ □ | □ ●

# Patterns with squares

Draw the shape that should come next in each pattern. In the table, count and write down the number of little squares needed to build each shape. Can you discover a pattern from the numbers in the table? Write the 5th number in the pattern.

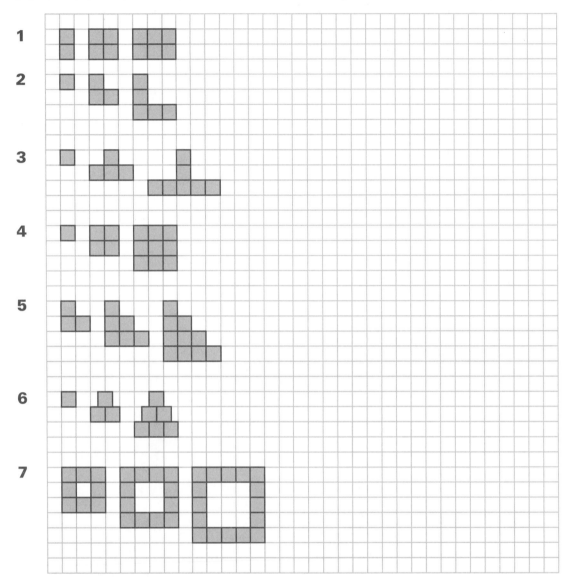

Number of squares in each shape

| | 1st shape | 2nd shape | 3rd shape | 4th shape | 5th shape |
|---|---|---|---|---|---|
| 1 | 2 | 4 | 6 | | |
| 2 | 1 | 3 | | | |
| 3 | 1 | | | | |
| 4 | 1 | | | | |
| 5 | | | | | |
| 6 | | | | | |
| 7 | | | | | |

# Faces

**1** Here is a face.

The eyes are open.
The mouth is happy.
The hair is curly.

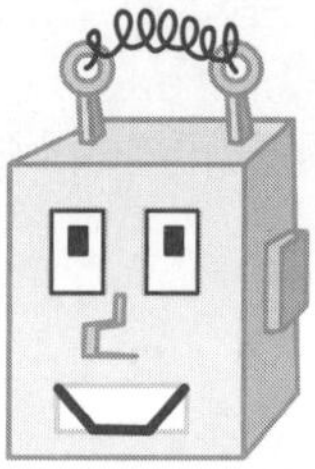

| | |
|---|---|
| Now both eyes are open | 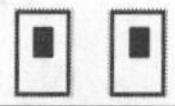 |
| but they could be closed |  |
| The hair is curly | 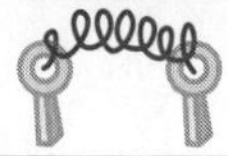 |
| but it could be straight | 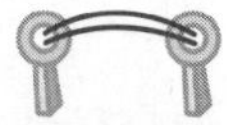 |
| The mouth is happy | 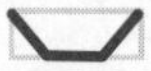 |
| but it could be sad | 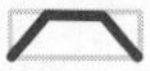 |
| or normal | 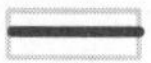 |

It is possible to make twelve different faces by combining these features in different ways. Can you draw them all?

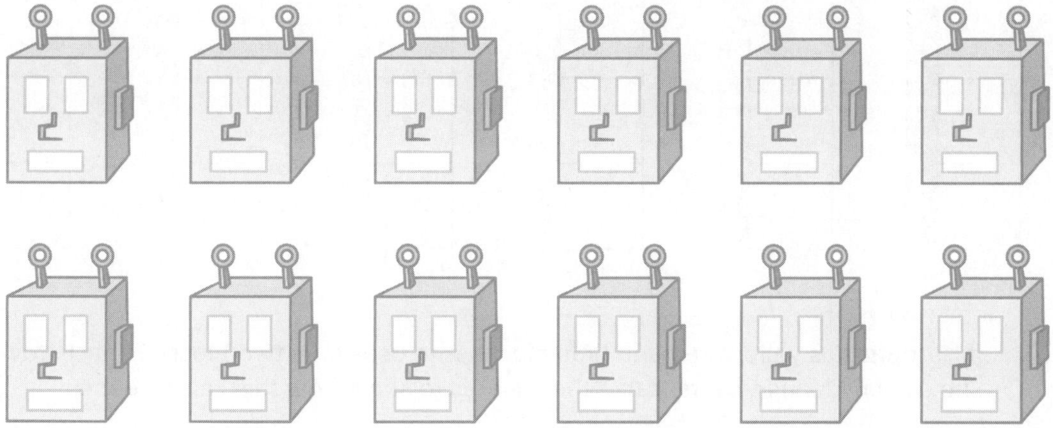

**2** The face can be different again.

Can you draw twelve different faces this time?

| | |
|---|---|
| The mouth can be happy | 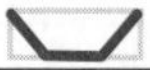 |
| or angry | 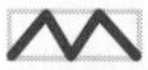 |
| The eyes can look straight | 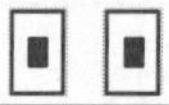 |
| or look up | 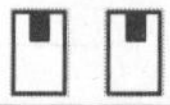 |
| or look down | 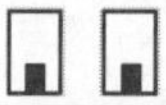 |
| The hair can be spikey | 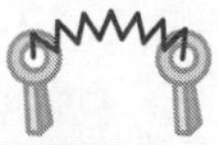 |
| or messy | 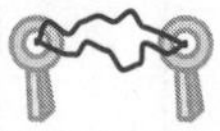 |

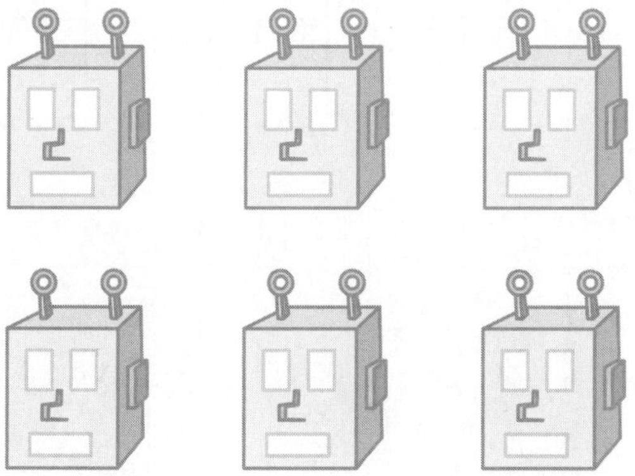

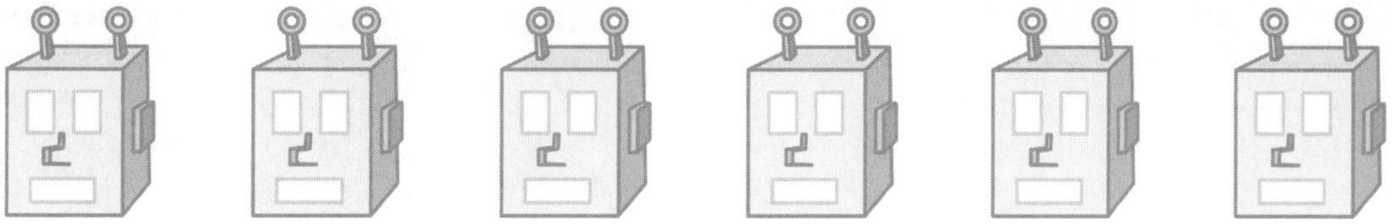

# Building blocks

**1** Toddler Harriette is building towers with her toy blocks. If she has only yellow and red blocks, and each tower contains three blocks, she can build eight different towers.

Here are two solutions: **Y** = yellow; **R** = red

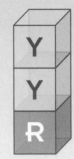

Now show the other six solutions.

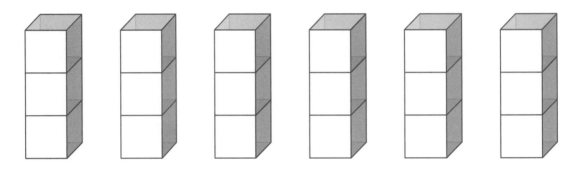

**2** If Harriette has yellow, red and blue blocks, and uses only two blocks in each tower, she can build nine towers. Label the squares to show how this can be done.

**Y** = yellow; **R** = red; **B** = blue

# Shading circles

When a circle is divided into two equal parts (halves), each half is called a semicircle.

**1**   In this exercise, each semicircle must be either shaded in one of two ways,

Two possible solutions are  and .

**Note:** Circles shaded like this are *not* considered to be different.

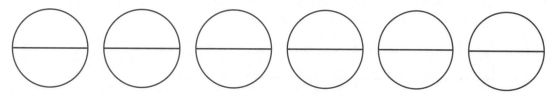

Can you shade six circles so that they are all different?

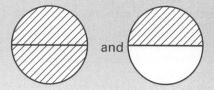

**2**   If you add another type of shading, so that the semicircles can be

Can you shade ten circles in ten different ways?

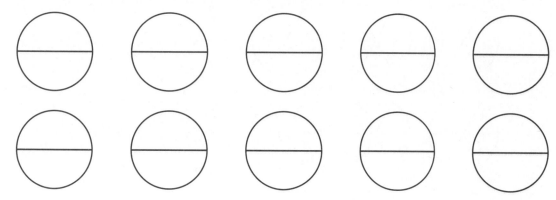

# Shading sectors

If you colour in two of the sectors of a circle that has been cut into six equal sectors, you can make the following patterns:

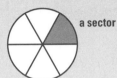 a sector

Remember that the circles can be turned around, so any other pattern you make will be the same as one of these when it is turned.

**1** Now colour in three of six equal sectors. Can you make three different patterns?

**2** Suppose a circle is cut into quarters. How many patterns can you make by either shading the quarters or leaving them white? Start with four white quarters, then shade one, and so on, working systematically.

**3** Now do the same with circles that again are divided into six sectors.

Working systematically, as in question 2, and starting with six white sectors, shade first one and then two, and so on. Altogether you should be able to make thirteen patterns.

# Colour these flags

**1** Can you colour these flags in six different ways, using the colours red, blue and yellow, if each colour can be used only once on each flag?

**2** Using flags with three stripes, as in question 1, how many different combinations can you make with the colours red, blue and yellow, if each colour can be used once, twice or three times in each flag?

Three possible combinations are shown at the right.

**3** Can you colour these flags in 24 different ways, using the colours red, blue, green and white, if each colour can be used only once on each flag?

# Chance

**1**   Colour in each spinner so that:

    **a**   there is 1 in 3 chance that it is red.

    **b**   there is 3 in 4 chance that it is yellow.

    **c**   there is 3 in 8 chance that it is green.

**2**   Colour in each hexagonal spinner so that:

    **a**   i
t is most likely to land on red.

    **b**   it is impossible that it lands on red.

    **c**   there is 1 chance in 6 it lands on red.

**3**   Allon spins the pointer on this spinner.

    **a**   What is the probability of spinning a 3? _____

    **b**   What is the probability of spinning an even number? _____

    **c**   What is the probability of spinning a number less than 4? _____

    **d**   What is the probability of spinning a number greater than 5? _____

**4**   Arrange the colours in order from most to least likely.

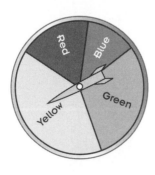

_____ Most likely

_____

_____

_____ Least likely

# How many routes?

**1**  Amelia lives at point A. Her school, four blocks away, is at S. She can use six different routes to walk the four blocks to school. Show each possible route on the figures below.

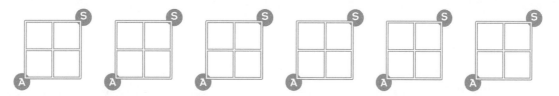

**2**  Raymond lives at point R. His school is five blocks away, at S. He can use ten different routes to walk the five blocks to school. One of the possible routes is drawn for you. Can you show the other nine ways?

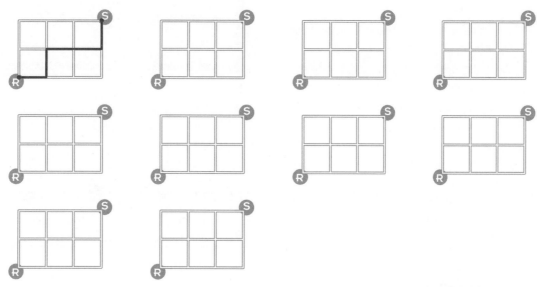

**3**  Visitors to Karen's flower garden must start at IN and leave at OUT. Draw in red all the routes visitors can take if they visit every flowerbed once and they all go first to the gladioli.

# Vegetable patch

**1** Mr White has planted vegetables in the garden shown below. Use the information given to work out the exact location of each vegetable patch if you are at the back of the garden. Use the abbreviations given to place your answer in the following diagram.

- The tomatoes (T) are in the right patch, third from the back.
- The zucchinis (Z) are to the left of the tomatoes (T) and behind the peas (P).
- The mushrooms (M) are behind the onions (O), while the onions (O) are behind the zucchinis (Z).
- The carrots (C) are next to the peas (P).
- The carrots (C) are in front of the tomatoes (T).
- The lettuce (L) are third from the front.
- The spinach (S) is next to the lettuce (L) and mushrooms (M).
- The onions (O) are to the left of the lettuce (L).

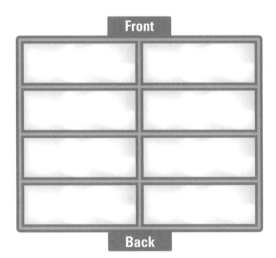

**2** Mr White would like his gardener to plant the flowers as shown. Describe the position of each flower patch in this garden so that the gardener will know where to plant each type of flower. You may use the first letter of each flower in your instruction. Test your instructions on your neighbour.

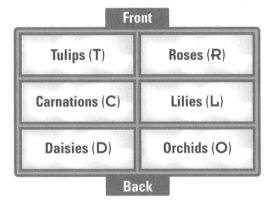

- _____
- _____
- _____
- _____
- _____
- _____

Chance & Data

# Graphs

**1**   This picture graph represents the number of people visiting a museum on a certain day, where ☺ = 20 people.

| Time | Number of people |
|------|------------------|
| 10 a.m.–11 a.m. | ☺ ☺ |
| 11 a.m.–12 noon | ☺ ☺ ☺ |
| 12 noon–1 p.m. | ☺ ☺ |
| 1 p.m.–2 p.m. | ☺ ☺ |
| 2 p.m.–3 p.m. | ☺ ☺ ☺ ☺ |
| 3 p.m.–4 p.m. | ☺ ☺ ☺ ☺ |

**a**   At what time did most people visit the museum?  _____

**b**   At what time did fewest people visit the museum?  _____

**c**   How many people were visiting between 10 a.m. and 11 a.m.?  _____

**d**   At what time did 60 people visit the museum?  _____

**e**   At which two times did the same
number of people visit the museum?  _____  _____

**f**   How many people visited after 3 p.m.?  _____

**g**   How many people visited the museum altogether?  _____

**h**   If it costs $2 to enter the museum how much was collected?  _____

**2**   On this graph, Gary's weight and height are represented by point G.

Place points on the graph that could represent:

**a**   Alex, who is taller but weighs
less than Gary (with A).

**b**   Bill, who is the same height as
Gary but is heavier (with B).

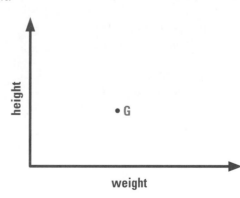

# Working with graphs

**1** Simon drew a graph of the height of a plant he bought.

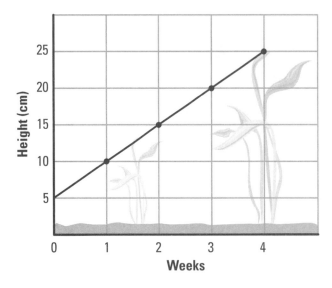

**a** What was the height of the plant when he bought it? _____

**b** How much did it grow in 4 weeks? _____

**c** How high do you think the plant will be at the end of 5 weeks? _____

**2** This sector graph shows the distribution of 60 prizes won at speech day.

**a** How many prizes were academic? _____

**b** How many prizes were sport awards? _____

**3** If in this sector graph there were 12 sport awards:

**a** How many prizes were academic? _____

**b** How many prizes were awarded altogether? _____

# Temperature readings

Find and write down the temperature shown on each thermometer.
Shade the bubble for the highest reading in each group of four.

All measurements are in °C.

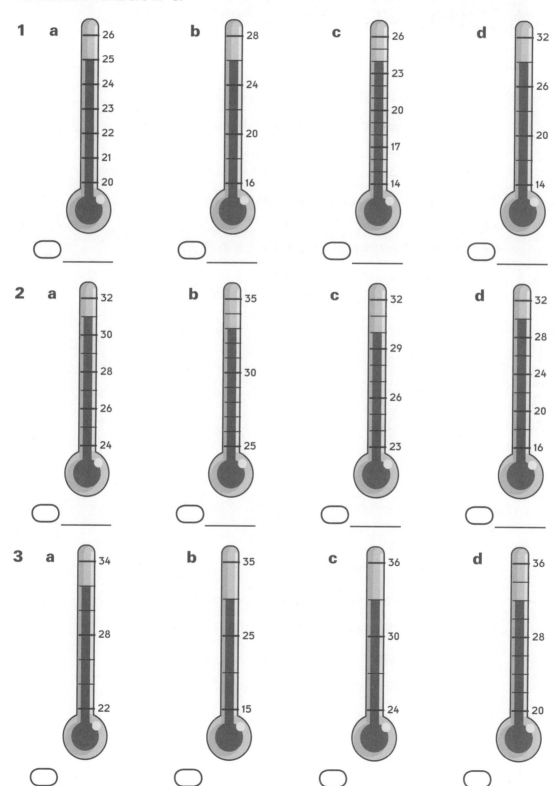

**1** **a** 26 25 24 23 22 21 20

**b** 28 24 20 16

**c** 26 23 20 17 14

**d** 32 26 20 14

**2** **a** 32 30 28 26 24

**b** 35 30 25

**c** 32 29 26 23

**d** 32 28 24 20 16

**3** **a** 34 28 22

**b** 35 25 15

**c** 36 30 24

**d** 36 28 20

# Temperature challenges

**1** On a certain day, the temperature was recorded at exactly every hour in both Melbourne and Sydney.

| Time | 8:00 a.m. | 9:00 a.m. | 10:00 a.m. | 11:00 a.m. | 12 noon |
|------|-----------|-----------|------------|------------|---------|
| Sydney | 18°C | 20°C | 21°C | 26°C | 30°C |
| Melbourne | 11°C | 12°C | 16°C | 20°C | 25°C |

**a** During which hour did the temperature rise most in Sydney? _____

**b** During which hour did the temperature rise most in Melbourne? _____

**c** What was the range of temperature in Sydney? _____
(The range is the difference between the lowest and highest temperature.)

**d** What was the range of temperature in Melbourne? _____

**e** What was the difference in
temperature between the two cities at 9:00 a.m.? _____

**f** During which hour was the difference
in temperature between the two cities the greatest? _____

**2** Study the temperature graph and use it to answer the questions below.

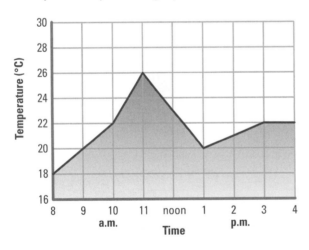

**a** At what time was the maximum temperature reached? _____

**b** What was the highest and lowest temperature recorded? _____

**c** Estimate the temperature at noon. _____

**d** During which hour did the temperature rise 4°C? _____

**e** When was the temperature 20°C? _____

**f** Describe in words what happened to the temperature between 8 a.m. and 4 p.m.?

_____

# Find the length

If AC = 12 cm and BC = 9 cm then we can see that AB = 3 cm.

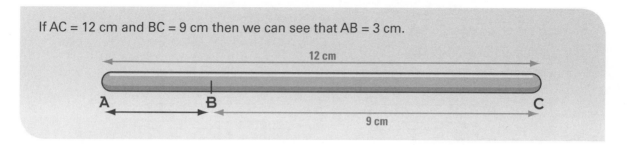

**1** In each of the following questions find the length of AB.

**a**

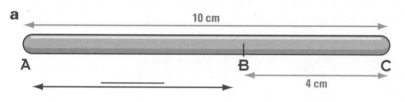

**b**

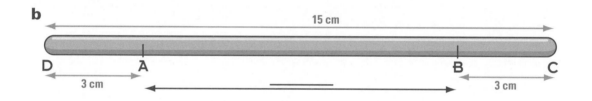

**c**

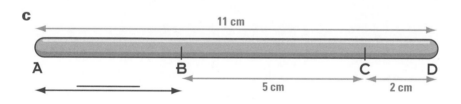

**d**

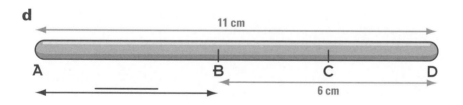

**2** Write down the lengths of the missing sides in each of the figures below.

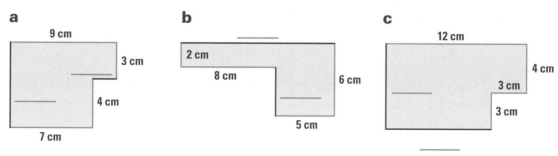

**a**
9 cm
3 cm
4 cm
7 cm

**b**
2 cm
8 cm
6 cm
5 cm

**c**
12 cm
4 cm
3 cm
3 cm

# Measuring lengths

Ben and his brother David had several toy building sticks.

The lengths of these sticks were 1 cm, 3 cm, 5 cm and 9 cm. The boys could measure a length of 2 cm and 4 cm using the 3 cm and 1 cm stick as shown below.

**1** Show that Ben and David can measure all the lengths from 1 cm to 18 cm with their sticks. Show each one on a diagram. Use a different colour for each size stick.

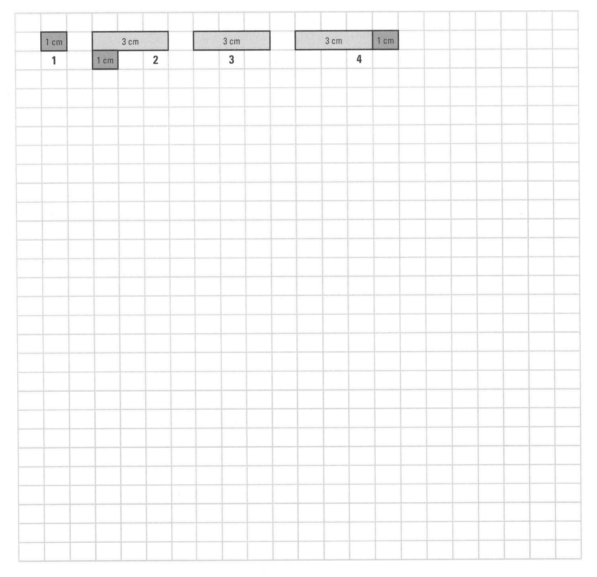

**2** Show that with sticks 1 cm, 3 cm, 7 cm and 15 cm long, Ben and David can measure all lengths up to 26 cm.

So that  5 = 7 + 1 – 3

6 = 7 – 1 and so on.

# How many tiles?

**1** 1 metre square tiles are placed all around a pool that measures 10 m by 4 m as shown. How many tiles are needed altogether? _____

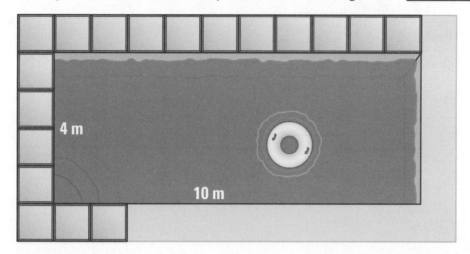

4 m

10 m

**2** A pathway (the shaded region) is built around a rectangular pool, as shown.

Work out the fewest number of tiles that can used in each question. You may need to draw the tiles carefully and count them.

**a** The pool is 5 metres by 8 metres, and the walkway is completely tiled with square tiles 1 metre by 1 metre. _____

**b** The pool is 8 metres by 10 metres, and the walkway is completely tiled with square tiles 2 metres by 2 metres. _____

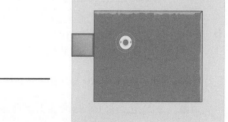

**c** The pool is 15 metres by 18 metres, and the walkway is completely tiled with square tiles 3 metres by 3 metres.

_____

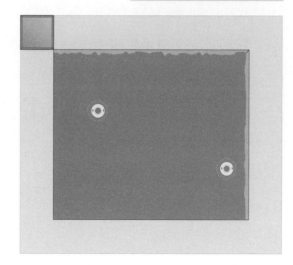

# Time puzzles

1   If today is Monday, what day of the week will it be:

   **a**   14 days from now?   _____

   **b**   28 days from now?   _____

   **c**   37 days from now?   _____

2   If two days ago it was Wednesday, what day of the week will it be:

   **a**   7 days from today?   _____

   **b**   21 days from today?   _____

   **c**   70 days from today?   _____

3   How many minutes are there in:

   **a**   $1\frac{1}{2}$ hours?   _____

   **b**   $3\frac{1}{4}$ hours?   _____

4   **a**   At my school, period one starts at 9:35 a.m. and lasts for 45 minutes.
          At what time will the bell ring for the end of this period?   _____

   **b**   It takes me 45 minutes to get to school from home.
          At what time should I leave in order to get to school at 8:30 a.m.?   _____

   **c**   A train left Sydney at 3:50 p.m. and arrived
          at Leura at 5:30 p.m. How long did the trip take?   _____

5   When Daniel wakes up, the clock is showing 7:05 a.m. What was the time at the end
   of each activity if it takes him:

   **a**   12 minutes to get dressed;   _____

   **b**   9 minutes to eat his breakfast;   _____

   **c**   6 minutes to clean his room;   _____

   **d**   25 minutes to practise his clarinet;   _____   and

   **e**   20 minutes to travel to school?   _____

   **f**   Daniel was supposed to be at school by 8:30 a.m. for band practice.
          How much time did he have before the practice started?   _____

6   Claudine's birthday is on 6 September. What will the date be:

   **a**   25 days after her birthday?   _____

   **b**   60 days after her birthday?   _____

# Time challenges

1   Put the following in the correct order.

   **a**   July, March, February, September   _____

   **b**   Wednesday, Sunday, Tuesday, Saturday   _____

   **c**   Summer, winter, spring, autumn   _____

2   Write down the correct time if the digital clock showing        is:

   **a**   3 minutes slow   _____

   **b**   7 minutes slow   _____

   **c**   8 minutes fast.   _____

3   The alarm at the Wong family home came on accidentally.

   **a**   It rang for 2 minutes and 25 seconds.
      For how many seconds was the alarm ringing?   _____

   **b**   If the alarm rang for 110 seconds, for
      how many minutes and seconds was it ringing?   _____

4   **a**   Stephanie walks 30 metres in 20 seconds. If she walks
      at the same speed, how far will she walk in 3 minutes?   _____

   **b**   When Joanne has a shower, she uses 3 litres of water
      every 15 seconds. How much water is used by a 5 minute shower?   _____

5   If the 1:30 p.m. train is 40 minutes late and the
   2:45 p.m. train is 12 minutes early, how minutes are they apart?   _____

6   Five planes leave an airport at equal intervals.
   The first plane leaves at 10 a.m. and the last plane
   leaves at 11 a.m. At what time does the fourth plane leave?   _____

7   Television advertisements run for 15 seconds, 30 seconds or 45 seconds.

   **a**   A set of advertisements is to run for 1 minute. One possibility is to have two
      30-second advertisements. Write down three other advertisement combinations
      of different lengths that could be used for this set.

      _____   _____

      _____

   **b**   A set of advertisements is to run for $1\frac{1}{2}$ minutes. One possibility is to have three
      30-second advertisements. Write down three other advertisement combinations
      of different lengths that could be used for this set.

      _____   _____

      _____

# Train timetable

Part of a train timetable is shown below:

| | | |
|---|---|---|
| **Beauty Point** | 7:15 | 7:28 |
| **Claireville** | 7:19 | 7:32 |
| **Pinner** | 7:24 | 7:37 |
| **Middletown** | 7:29 | 7:42 |
| **Viewpoint** | 7:34 | 7:47 |
| **Bellevue Hill** | 7:40 | 7:53 |

**1**   If Edwina catches the train at Claireville at 7:19,
how long is her journey if she gets off the train at Bellevue Hill?   _____

**2**   Darren arrived at Beauty Point Station at 7:17 missing the 7:15
train by 2 minutes. How long will he have to wait for the next train?   _____

**3**   How long is the trip from Beauty Point to Bellevue Hill?   _____

**4**   Lillian arrived at Middletown station at 7:35.

    **a**   How long will she have to wait for the next train?   _____

    **b**   What time will she arrive at Viewpoint?   _____

**5**   Nathan had to meet a friend at 7:40 at Viewpoint Station. At what
time should he catch the train from Beauty Point to be there on time?   _____

**6**   If Matthew just misses the train at Pinner Station
at 7:24, how long will he have to wait for the next train?   _____

# Read the dial

How much fuel is in each tank if the capacity is given in each case?

**1**  **a** _____  **b** _____  **c** _____

40 L

40 L

40 L

**2**  **a** _____  **b** _____  **c** _____

60 L

60 L

80 L

**3**  **a** _____  **b** _____  **c** _____

36 L

80 L

36 L

**4**  **a** _____  **b** _____  **c** _____

50 L

100 L

100 L

# Weighing parcels

There are two different types of parcels being weighed in kilograms on each set of scales. Write down the mass shown on the first two scales. Work out the mass of the parcel on the set of scales on the right and draw the pointer on the scales to show this mass.

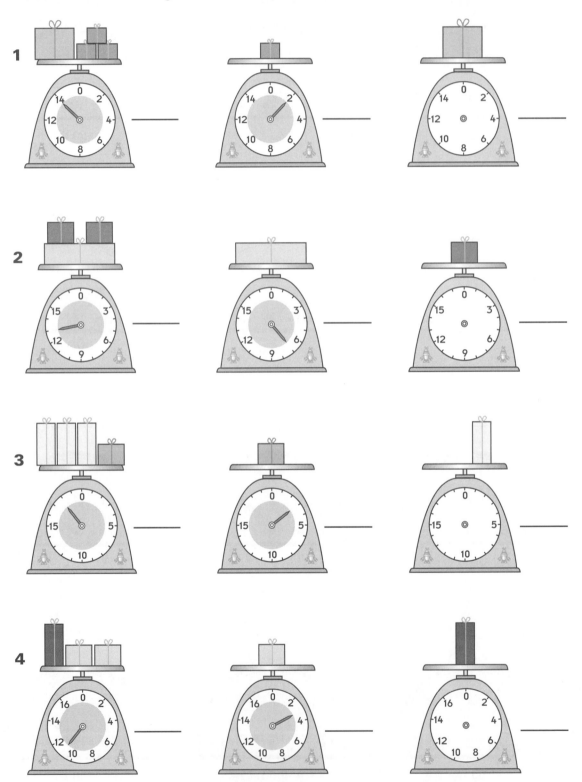

# Mass problem solving

**1** Larri's mass is 4 kg more than Rhonda's. The sum of their masses is 38 kg. What is the mass of each person?

| Larri's mass | Rhonda's mass | The sum |
|---|---|---|
|  |  | 38 kg |

**2** Veronica's mass is 3 kg less than Damien's. The sum of their masses is 51 kg. What is the mass of each person?

| Veronica's mass | Damien's mass | The sum |
|---|---|---|
|  |  |  |

**3** Together a book and a parcel have a mass of 10 kg. The parcel has a mass 6 kg more than the book. What is the mass of each?

| Mass of parcel | Mass of book | Total mass |
|---|---|---|
|  |  |  |

**4** Peter and Daniel both buy fruit. Peter buys 3 kg more than Daniel. Together they buy 17 kg. How many kilograms of fruit does each man buy?

| Daniel's fruit | Peter's fruit | Total mass of fruit |
|---|---|---|
|  |  |  |

**5** Together a drink and a banana have a mass of 500 g. The drink has a mass of 100 g more than the banana. What is the mass of each?

| Mass of banana | Mass of drink | Total mass |
|---|---|---|
|  |  |  |

**6** Together an apple and a pear have a mass of 600 g. The apple has a mass 100 g more than the pear. What is the mass of each?

| Mass of apple | Mass of pear | Total mass |
|---|---|---|
|  |  |  |

**7** Together a pear and a pineapple have a mass of 2 kg. The pineapple has a mass 9 times that of the pear. What is the mass of each?

| Mass of pear | Mass of pineapple | Total mass |
|---|---|---|
|  |  |  |

# Find the mass

Find the mass of each object being measured.

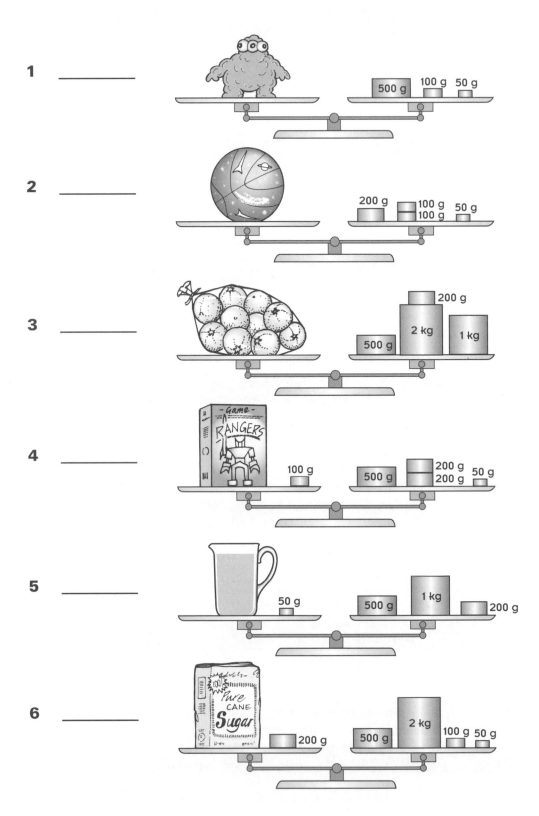

1 _____

2 _____

3 _____

4 _____

5 _____

6 _____

# Travelling

**1** Jamie and Amelia were driving and came across this sign on the road.

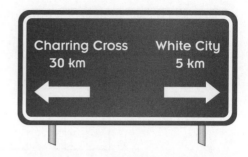

   **a** How far apart are Charring Cross and White City? _____

   **b** When they see this second sign how far have they travelled along this road? _____

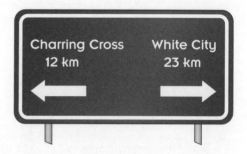

   **c** Towards which city were they travelling?

   _____

After reading the above sign Jamie and Amelia turn back and travel towards White City.

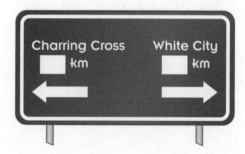

   **d** After travelling for 10 km they see another sign. Complete this sign at the right.

**2** When Jamie and Amelia reached White City they went shopping in a big shopping centre. Amelia parked her car on P3 and they got into the lift.

   **a** If Amelia had to go to level 4, how many floors did they go up? _____

   **b** When Jamie got into the lift on P3 it went up 6 floors and then down 2 floors. On which level did Jamie get out? _____

   **c** Amelia's daughter Vera loves playing in the lift. They got in at level 1, went up 6 levels, down 9 levels, then up 4 levels. On which floor did they end up? _____

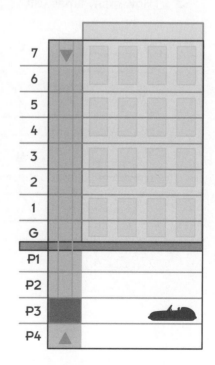

# Count the shapes

To solve these puzzles, first draw dotted lines in the figures, then count the shapes.

**1** How many times will  fit into each of these figures?

**a** _____ **b** _____ **c** _____ **d** _____ **e** _____ **f** _____

**2**  will fit twice into  and this can be done in two ways: or

How many times will  fit into each of these figures?

**a** _____ **b** _____ **c** _____ **d** _____ **e** _____

 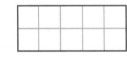  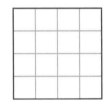 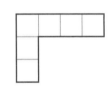

**3** How many times will  fit into each of these figures?

**a** _____ **b** _____ **c** _____ **d** _____ **e** _____

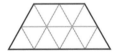 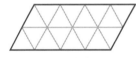  

**f** _____ **g** _____ **h** _____

# Counting cubes

**1**  Count the number of little cubes that have been stacked to form these figures. **Remember to count the cubes that you cannot see.** It would be a good idea to build the figures, using little cubes.

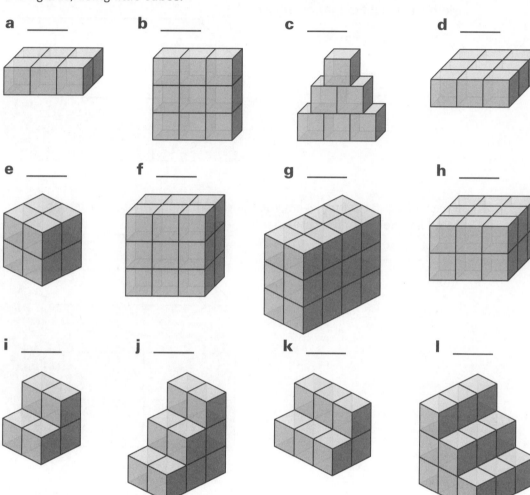

a _____    b _____    c _____    d _____

e _____    f _____    g _____    h _____

i _____    j _____    k _____    l _____

**2**  This large cube, 3 × 3 × 3, is made up of 27 little cubes.
How many little cubes must be removed from it to make each of the figures below?

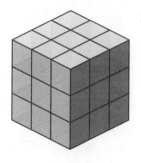

a _____    b _____    c _____

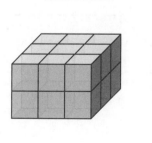
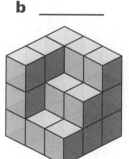
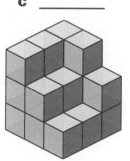

Check each answer by removing the little cubes from your large cube.

# Packing boxes

**1**   Twelve boxes are placed inside this container.

   **a**   If each box is 8 cm long, 3 cm wide and 2 cm high, what is the length, width and height of the container?

      l = _____ cm

      w = _____ cm

      h = _____ cm

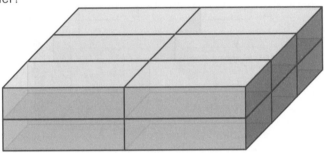

   **b**   If each box is 6 cm long, 4 cm wide and 3 cm high, what is the length, width and height of the container?

      l = _____ cm

      w = _____ cm

      h = _____ cm

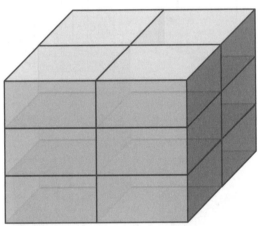

**2**   This container is 6 cm long, 4 cm wide and 2 cm high.

   **a**   How many 1 cm cubes can be placed inside this container?   _____

   **b**   How many 2 cm cubes can be placed inside this container?   _____

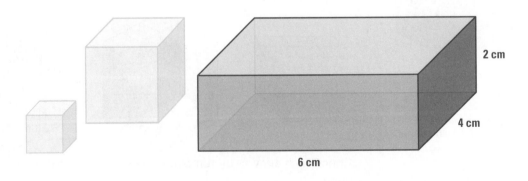

2 cm

4 cm

6 cm

# Rolling boxes

Imagine that the first box in each of these exercises is rolled to the right, *end over end*, so that the symbol on it is always facing towards you. In the first exercise, for example, the box will be turned four times.

In each exercise, draw the symbol as it would look at each turn of the box. To carry out an experiment, cut out an identical shape and draw the symbol on it.

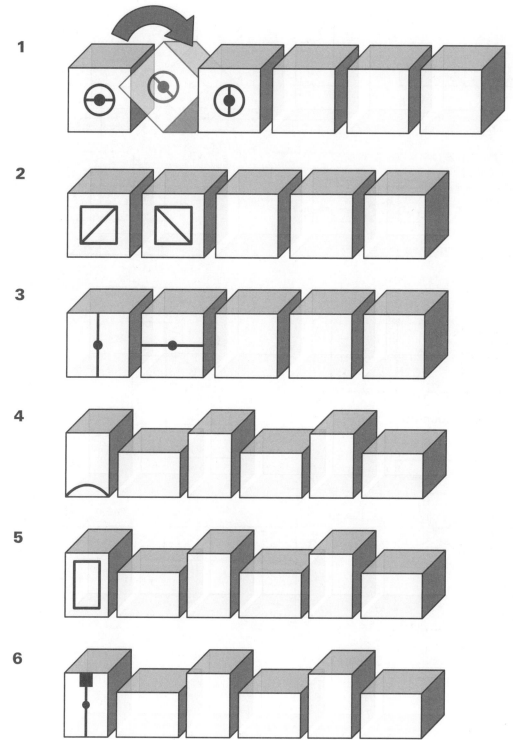

# Torn rectangles

Eight rectangles were drawn on squared paper that was then accidently torn.

How many little squares made up each original rectangular shape before it was torn?

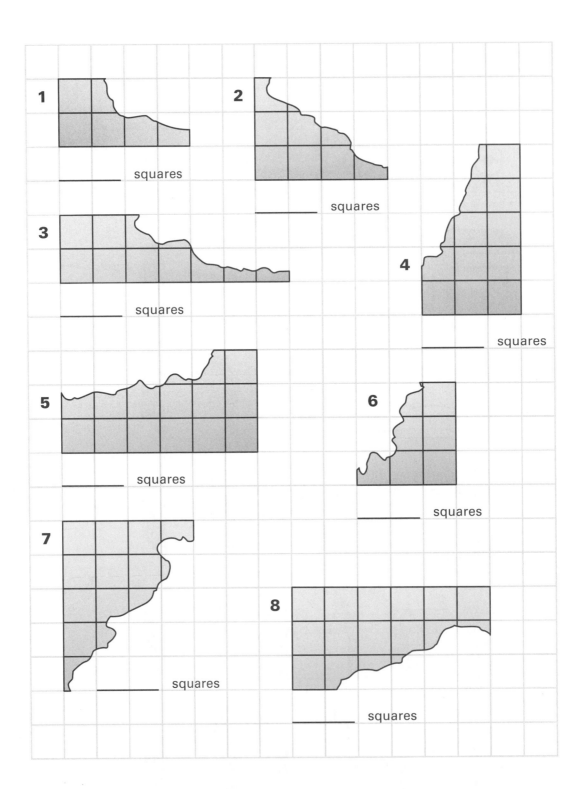

1 _____ squares

2 _____ squares

3 _____ squares

4 _____ squares

5 _____ squares

6 _____ squares

7 _____ squares

8 _____ squares

# Position

**1** Below is part of the seating plan for a theatre showing (the white spaces) where some vacant seats are that can be bought. Five friends want to buy tickets for a show. Many of the seats are already sold. The seat (shaded in a different colour) for a disabled person is G6.

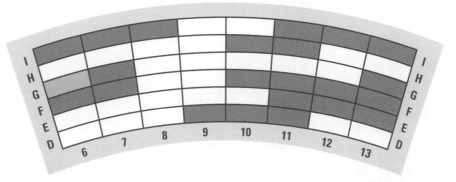

**a** Which 5 seats should the friends ask for if they want to sit next to each other?

_____ _____ _____ _____ _____

**b** Once they were in the theatre they noticed one of their school friends sitting all alone. What seat was this person sitting in? _____

**c** Later they noticed 4 boys from another school sitting together. What seats were these boys sitting in?

_____ _____ _____ _____

**2** Guess the cards. Four cards lie face down on the table:

The cards are not in the order given above, but the following facts are known about them.

- The card with ★ is to the left of the card with △.

- The card with ◯ is not on the edge, and is to the right of the ★.

- The card with △ is between the card with ● and the card with ◯.

What is the order of the cards?

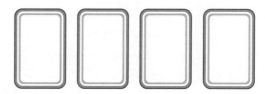

**3** A group of children stood in single file. If Dawn was sixth from either end, how many children were standing in the line? _____

**4** Place five children in order of size, from the smallest to the tallest, using information given in these statements:

- Gabriel is the same size as Asher, but taller than Niva.

- Asher is taller than Joel, but smaller than Emma.

- Niva is shorter than Joel.

_____

_____

_____

_____

_____

# Tessellations

Continue each of the tessellations by drawing more of the basic shapes.
Colour in your tessellations using two colours.

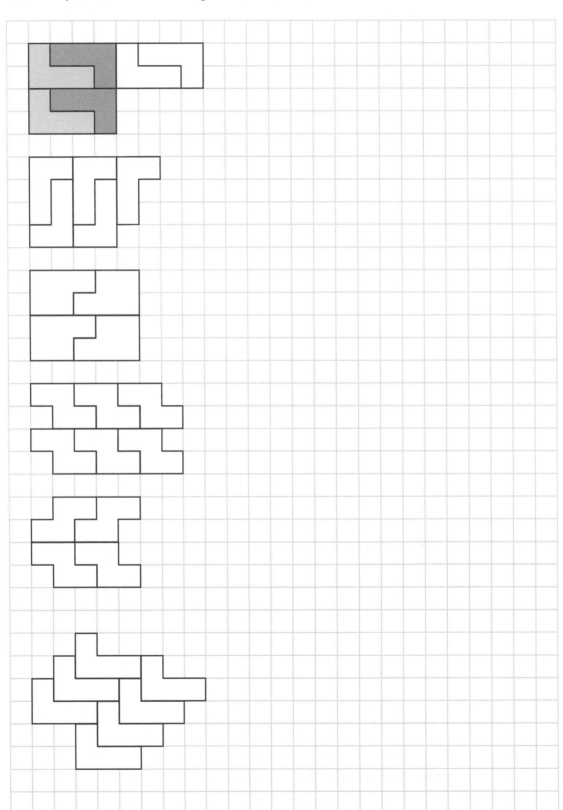

# Solid shapes

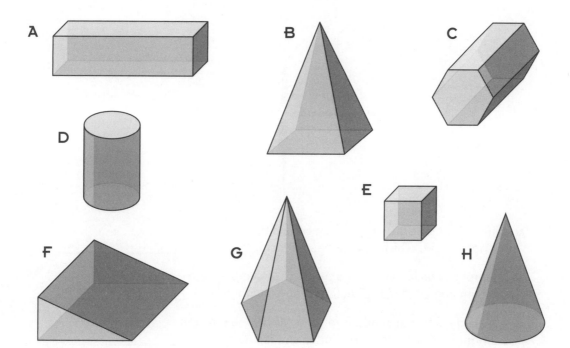

**1** Can you name each of the solids above?

A _____     B _____

C _____     D _____

E _____     F _____

G _____     H _____

**2** Which of the solids has

   **a** the smallest number of vertices?     _____

   **b** the largest number of faces?     _____

   **c** the smallest number of faces?     _____

   **d** six vertices?     _____

   **e** three rectangular faces?     _____

   **f** five triangular faces?     _____

**3** How many faces has solid G?     _____

**4** How many edges has solid A?     _____

**5** How many vertices has solid B?     _____

# Bearings

**1**

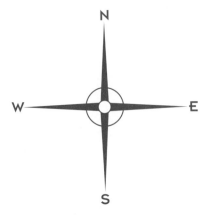

**a** Ian is facing north. He turns clockwise through 1 right angle. Which direction is he facing now? _____

**b** Simone is facing west. She turns clockwise through 3 right angles. Which direction is she facing now? _____

**c** Melinda is facing south. She turns clockwise through 2 right angles. Which direction is she facing now? _____

**2**

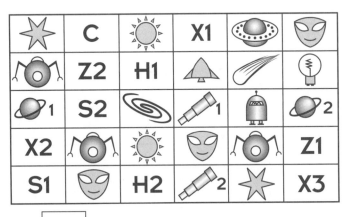
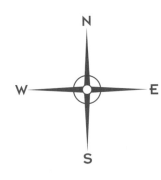

Each ☐ is a block. To walk from **S1** to **S2**, you need to walk 1 block east then 2 blocks north or 2 blocks north, and then 1 block east. In each question below state how many blocks and in which direction the person had to walk.

**a** Bob was at **H1** and wanted to walk to **H2**. _____

**b** Eli was at 🪐1 and wanted to walk to 🪐2. _____

**c** Jan was at **X1** and wanted to walk to **X2** and from **X2** to **X3**.

_____

**d** Harry is at **C** and wanted to walk to ✦. _____

**e** Kerry is at the north-east corner of this diagram at 👽 and

wanted to walk to 🔭2. _____

# Challenging cubes

**1**

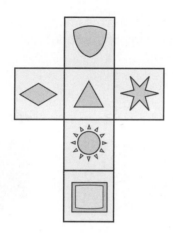

When this net is folded into a cube, which shape:

**a** is opposite  ?

**b** is opposite  ?

**c** is not next to  ?

**d** If the net above is folded to make a cube, draw two different views we could see if  was on the top.

**e** If the net above is folded to make a cube, draw two different views we could see if  was on the top.

**2** Here are four views of one cube.

**a** What are the shapes on the faces adjacent to (next to)  ?

Now work out which shape is on the face opposite  .

**b** What are the shapes on the faces adjacent to  ?

What shape is on the face opposite  ?

**c** What shape is on the face opposite  ?

space

# Painting solids

Small white cubes are glued together to make a solid shape. All the outside faces of this solid are then painted blue. In each example work out how many of the cubes have a certain number of blue faces.

**1**    How many of the cubes have only:

     4 blue faces = _____

     3 blue faces = _____

     Total cubes = _____

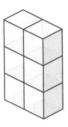 

**2**    How many of the cubes have only:

     4 blue faces = _____

     3 blue faces = _____

     2 blue faces = _____

     Total cubes = _____

**3**    How many of the cubes have only:

     4 blue faces = _____

     3 blue faces = _____

     2 blue faces = _____

     Total cubes = _____

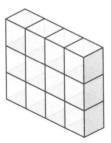

**4**    How many of the cubes have only:

     3 blue faces = _____

     2 blue faces = _____

     1 blue face= _____

     Total cubes = _____

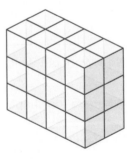

# How many blocks?

**1**  **a**  How many red blocks are needed to build Model A?  _____

    **b**  How many blue blocks are needed to fill in the inside of this shape?  _____

    **c**  How many yellow blocks need to be placed on top of
this shape now to make a rectangular block three layers deep?  _____

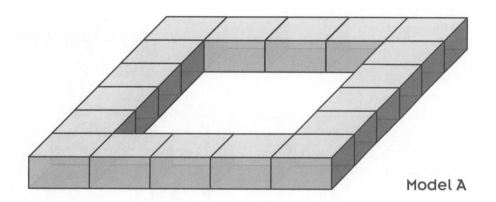

Model A

**2**  **a**  How many red blocks are needed to build Model B?  _____

    **b**  How many blue blocks are needed to fill in the inside of this shape?

        _____

    **c**  How many yellow blocks need to be placed on top of this
shape now to make a rectangular block four layers deep?  _____

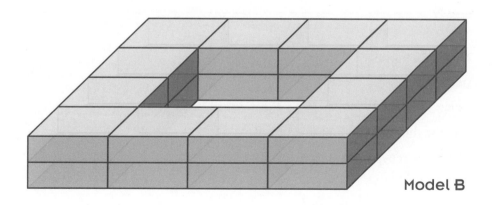

Model B

# Amazing mathematics

**1**   Think of a number.

Add 6.

Double the result.

Take away 4.

Halve the result.

Take away the number you
first thought of.

Try this with different numbers.
What have you found?

_____

_____

_____

_____

**2**   Think of a number.

Add 5.

Multiply the result by 3.

Subtract 9.

Divide that answer by 3 (that is, find $\frac{1}{3}$ of the answer).

Subtract 2.

Try this with different numbers. What have you found?

_____

**3**   Think of a number.

Double it.

Add 9.

Add the number you first thought of.

Divide the result by 3.

Add 2.

Subtract the original number.

Try this with different numbers. What have you found?

_____

# Logic using scales

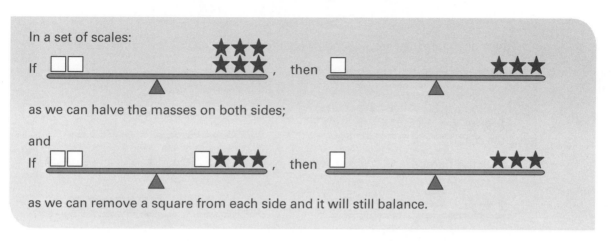

In a set of scales:

If ⬜⬜ ⭐⭐⭐/⭐⭐⭐ , then ⬜ ⭐⭐⭐

as we can halve the masses on both sides;

and

If ⬜⬜ ⬜⭐⭐⭐ , then ⬜ ⭐⭐⭐

as we can remove a square from each side and it will still balance.

For each of these sentences, work out what must be done to find the number of stars (⭐) needed to balance one square (⬜).

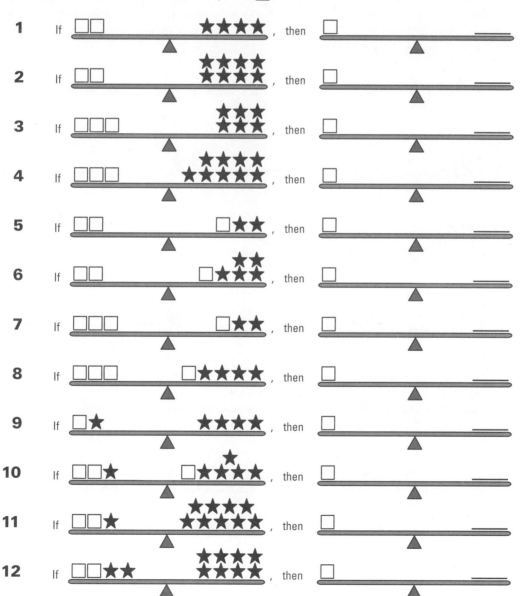

**1** If ⬜⬜ ⭐⭐⭐⭐ , then ⬜ ____

**2** If ⬜⬜ ⭐⭐⭐⭐/⭐⭐⭐⭐ , then ⬜ ____

**3** If ⬜⬜⬜ ⭐⭐⭐/⭐⭐⭐ , then ⬜ ____

**4** If ⬜⬜⬜ ⭐⭐⭐⭐/⭐⭐⭐⭐⭐ , then ⬜ ____

**5** If ⬜⬜ ⬜⭐⭐ , then ⬜ ____

**6** If ⬜⬜ ⬜⭐⭐⭐/⭐⭐ , then ⬜ ____

**7** If ⬜⬜⬜ ⬜⭐⭐ , then ⬜ ____

**8** If ⬜⬜⬜ ⬜⭐⭐⭐⭐ , then ⬜ ____

**9** If ⬜⭐ ⭐⭐⭐⭐ , then ⬜ ____

**10** If ⬜⬜⭐ ⬜⭐⭐⭐⭐/⭐ , then ⬜ ____

**11** If ⬜⬜⭐ ⭐⭐⭐⭐/⭐⭐⭐⭐⭐ , then ⬜ ____

**12** If ⬜⬜⭐⭐ ⭐⭐⭐⭐/⭐⭐⭐⭐ , then ⬜ ____

# Balanced scales

Work out how many stars (★) are needed to balance the scales in each of these sentences.

**Hint:** Draw some scales to help in your working.

**1** If ★★★★ ⬤⬤ , then ⬤⬤⬤

**2** If ★★★ ☐⬤ , then ☐☐☐⬤⬤⬤

**3** If ⬤★ ☐ and ★★★ ⬤ , then ☐

**4** If ★★☐ ⬤⬤ and ★★★ ☐ , then ⬤⬤

**5** If ⬤⬤ ☐ and ⬤ ★★ , then ☐

**6** If ★★★★★ ☐⬤ and ★★★ ☐ , then ⬤

**7** If ⬤⬤⬤ ☐★ and ⬤ ★ , then ☐

**8** If ⬤⬤⬤ ☐☐ and ★★ ⬤ , then ☐

**9** If ⬤⬤ ☐☐☐ and ★★★ ⬤ , then ☐

**10** If ⬤⬤ ☐☐★★ and ☐ ★★★ , then ⬤

# Shapes and symbols

Which shapes or symbols must be added to these squares in order to make the patterns complete?

**1**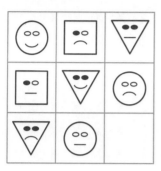

**2**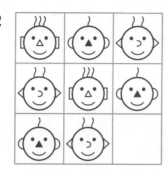

**3**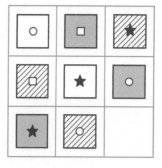

**4**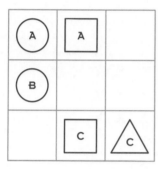

**5**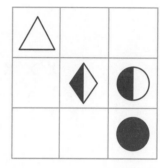

**6**

**7**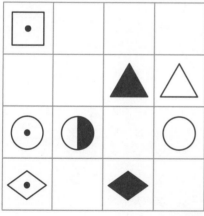

**8**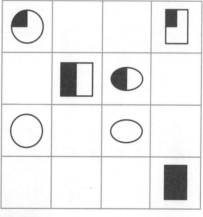

# How many?

How many **X**s are there in each diagram below?

**1**
```
X X X X X X X
X X X X X X X
X X X X X   X
X X X X     X
X X X       X
X X         X
X X X X X X X  _____
```

**2**
```
X X X X X X X X
X X X X X     X
X X X X X     X
X X X X X X X X
X     X X X X X
X     X X X X X
X X X X X X X X  _____
```

**3**
```
        X
      X X X
    X X X X X
  X X X X X X X
          X X X
          X X X X X
          X X X X X X X

          _____
```

**4**
```
          X X X X
            X X X X
          X X X X
            X X X X
        X X X X
        X X X
        X X
        X
                    _____
```

**5**
```
X X X X X X X X X
  X X X X X X X X X
X   X X X X X     X
X       X X X     X
X   X X   X X     X
X X X         X X X
X X             X X
X X X X X X X X X X
                    _____
```

**6**
```
        X X
      X X X X X
    X X X X X X
    X X X       X
    X X X
    X X X
    X X X         X
    X X X X X X X
      X X X X X
        X X        _____
```

# Shaded figures

The values of the shaded sections are given in these squares.

   Find the values of all the other sections, and finally write the value of each large square underneath it.

**1** 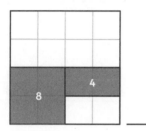 ____

**2** 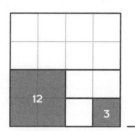 ____

**3** 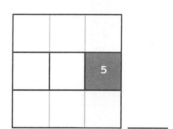 ____

**4** 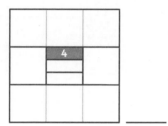 ____

**5** 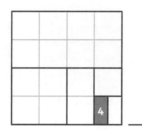 ____

**6** 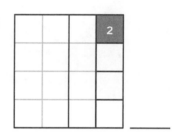 ____

**7** 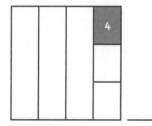 ____

**8** 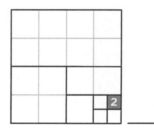 ____

**9** 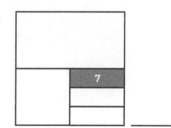 ____

**10** 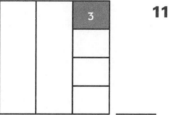 ____

**11** 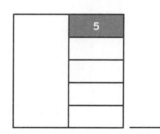 ____

**12** 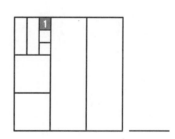 ____

**13** 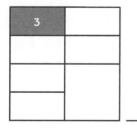 ____

**14** 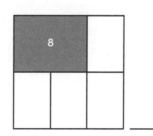 ____

**15** 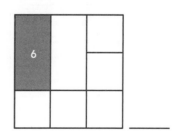 ____

# Shaded values

The values of the shaded sections are given in these squares. Find the values of all the other sections, and finally write the value of each large square underneath it.

**1**

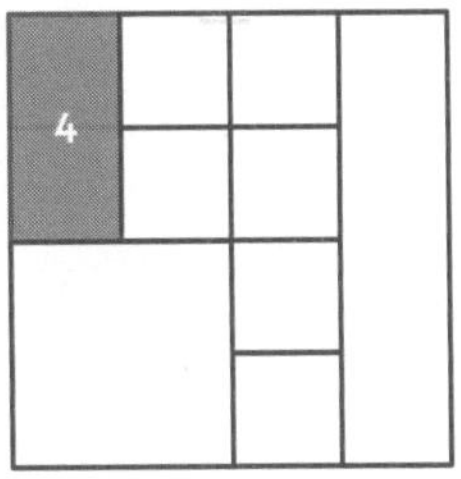

4

**2**

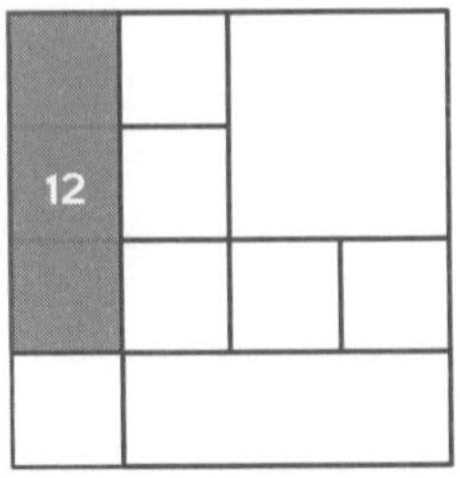

12

**3**

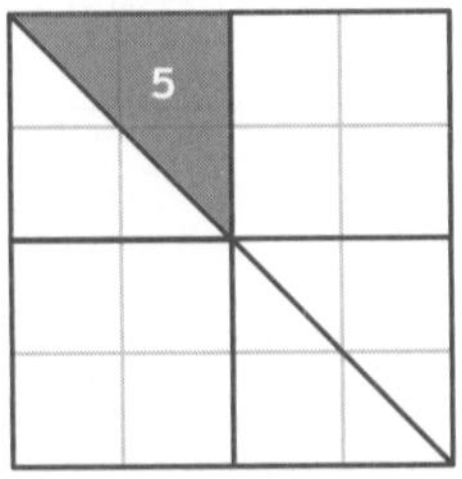

5

**4**

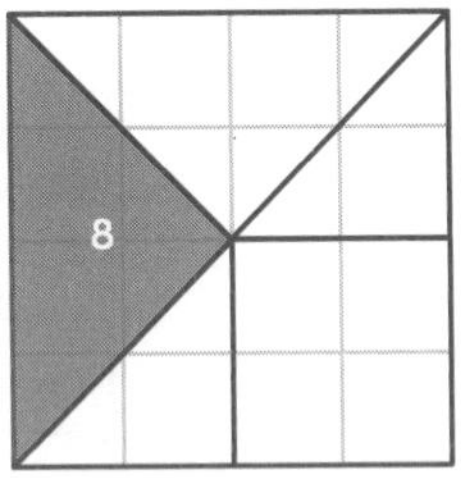

8

**5**

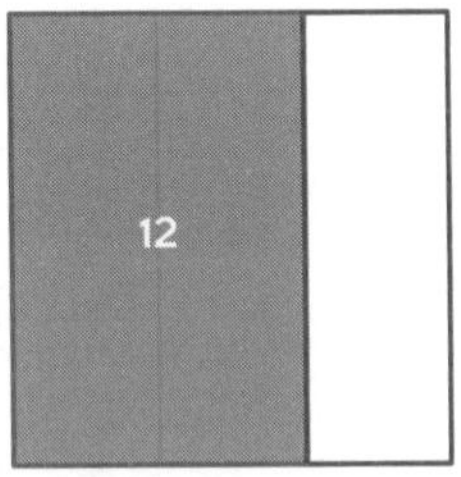

12

**6**

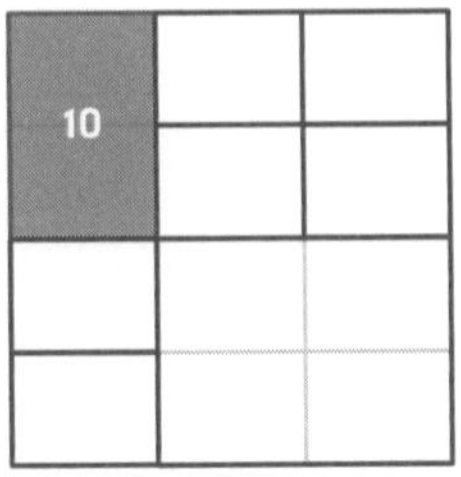

10

**7**

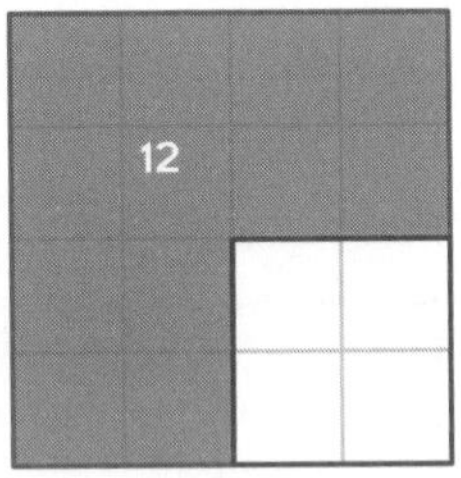

12

**8**

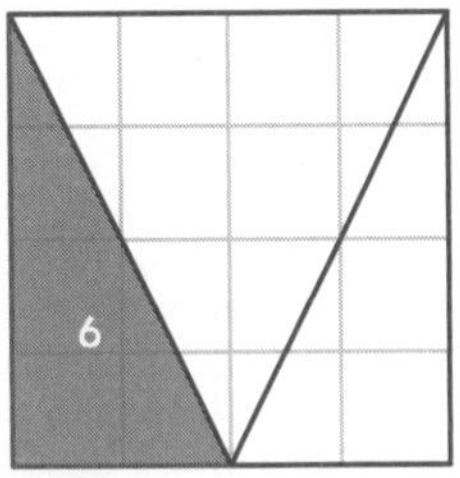

6

**9**

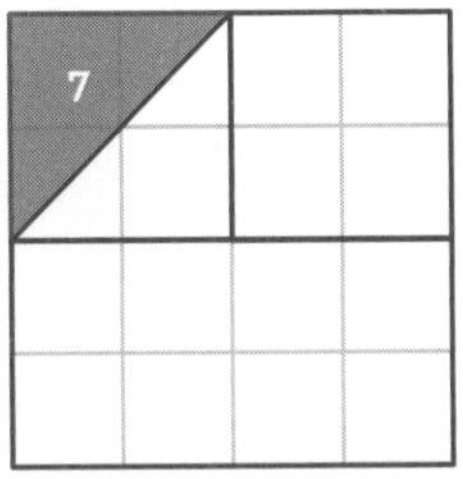

7

**10**

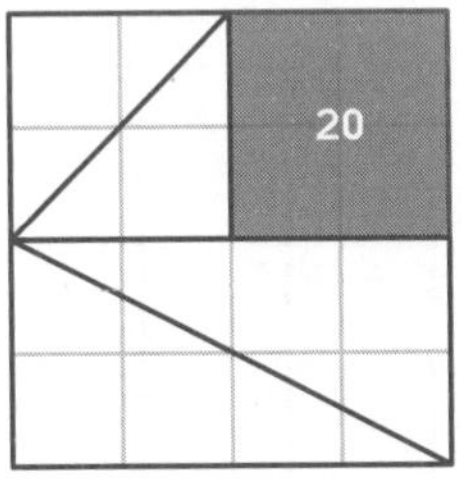

20

**11**

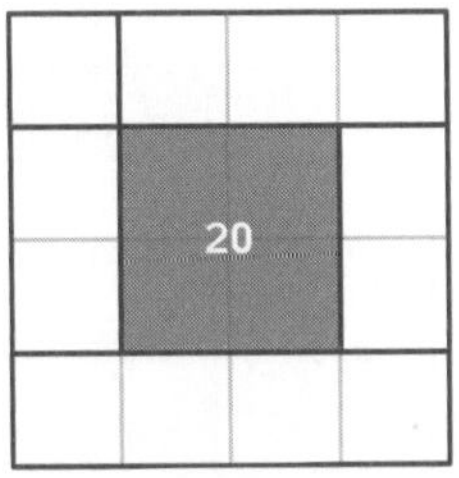

20

**12**

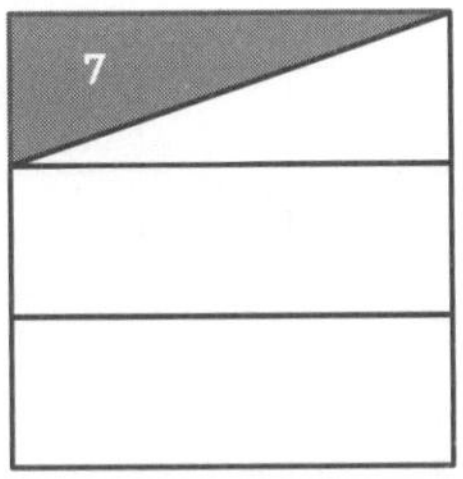

7

**13**

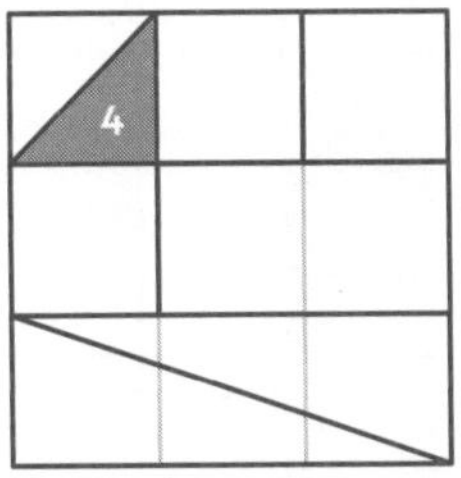

4

**14**

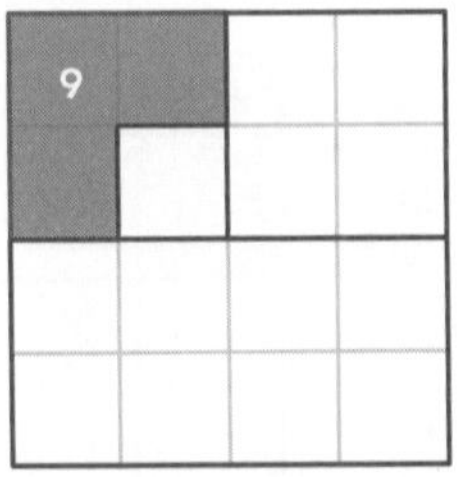

9

**15**

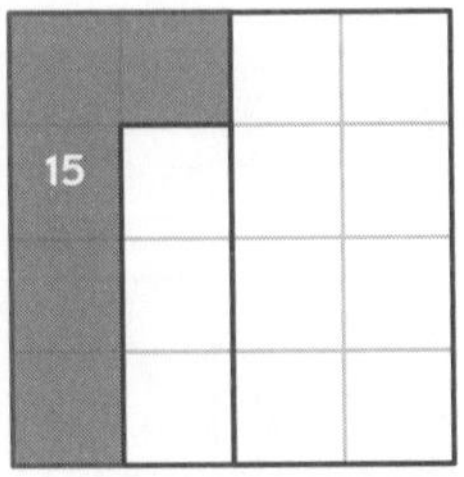

15

# Triangular numbers

The numbers 1, 3, 6 and 10 are called 'triangular numbers'. They are the numbers you get by adding the rows of dots in the triangles.

| 1 | 3 | 6 | 10 |
|---|---|---|---|
| 1 | 1 + 2 = 3 | 1 + 2 + 3 = 6 | 1 + 2 + 3 + 4 = 10 |

**1** Continuing the pattern of dots shown above, write down the next five triangular numbers.

_____  _____  _____  _____  _____

**2** Notice that a pattern can be seen in the differences when you take away one triangular number from the one above it.

1    3    6    10

2    3    4

3 − 1 = 2    6 − 3 = 3    10 − 6 = 4

By continuing the above pattern in the differences, build up the triangular numbers to the next six terms.

**3 a** When the Friendly Society meets, the members all shake hands. How many handshakes are exchanged? Complete the table on the right. Have you spotted the pattern?

**b** If 21 handshakes are exchanged, how many members are at the meeting? _____

**c** If 55 handshakes are exchanged, how many members are at the meeting? _____

| Members present | Handshakes |
|---|---|
| 2 | 1 |
| 3 | 3 |
| 4 | |
| 5 | |
| 6 | |
| 7 | |
| 8 | |
| 9 | |
| 10 | |
| 11 | |

# Joining the dots

**1** In each diagram, how many lines are needed to join each point to every other point? Make sure you count the lines **as you join each pair of points**.

  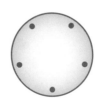  

Complete this table.

| Number of points | Number of lines |
|------------------|-----------------|
| 3 | 3 |
| 4 | 6 |
| 5 | |
| 6 | |
| 7 | |
| 8 | |
| 9 | |

**2** In a netball competition there are six teams. Each team plays one match against every other team.

**a** How many matches does each team play? _____

**b** How many matches are played altogether? Represent the teams with dots, as shown here. _____

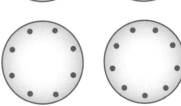

# How many triangles?

A triangle has been repeatedly folded through one of its vertices.

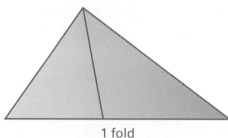

1 fold

With one fold, the result is 3 triangles:
2 small triangles and 1 double triangle.

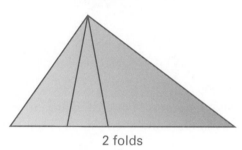

2 folds

With 2 folds, the result is 6 triangles:
3 small triangles, 2 double triangles and
1 triple triangle.

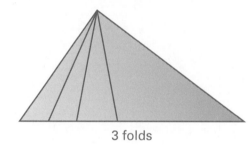

3 folds

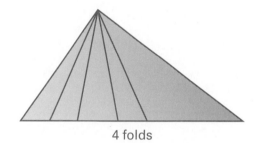

4 folds

**1** What is the total number of triangles formed? Remember to count the triangles systematically in each case: first, single; then double; then triple; then more than three, as needed in each case.

Complete this table. Try to discover the number pattern.

| Folds | 0 | 1 | 2 | 3 | 4 | 5 |
|---|---|---|---|---|---|---|
| Triangles (total) | 1 | 3 | 6 | | | |

**2** Can you predict the number of triangles there will be after 8 folds? _____

See *Teacher's Book* for diagram masters.

# Count the triangles

Study the example that shows you how to count the triangles in this diagram:
To make sure you count all the possible triangles,
you must work systematically.

The number of single triangles is 4:

There are 2
double triangles:

There are 2
triple triangles:

So the total number of triangles is 8.

How many triangles are there in each of the following diagrams? For each diagram, set out your work as shown above, counting the single triangles and shading the larger ones.

**1**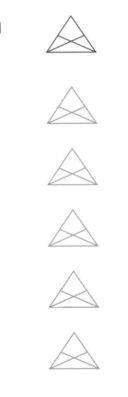

**2**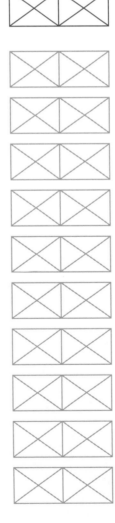

**3**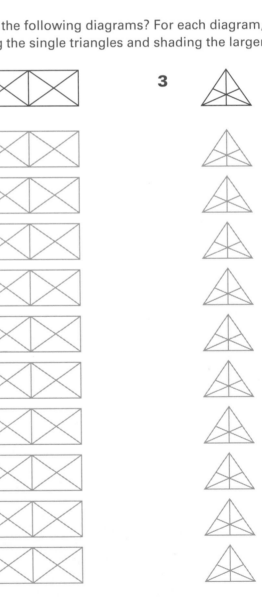

# Logic with figures

In each group of figures, C changes to D in the same way that A changes to B.

Draw the figure that E must change to in order to continue the pattern.

| | A | ➡ | B | | C | ➡ | D | | E | ➡ |
|---|---|---|---|---|---|---|---|---|---|---|

**1**  ➡   ➡

**2**

**3**

**4**

**5**

**6**

**7**

**8**

**9**

**10**

Working Mathematically

# Matchstick puzzles

Draw the next two diagrams in each pattern below and complete the table. Look for a pattern from which you can predict the number of matches needed for the tenth diagram.

**1**

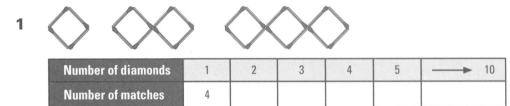

| Number of diamonds | 1 | 2 | 3 | 4 | 5 | → | 10 |
|---|---|---|---|---|---|---|---|
| Number of matches | 4 | | | | | | |

**2**

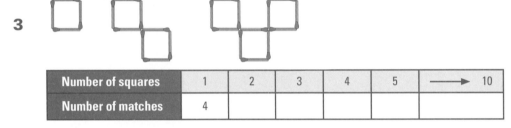

| Number of triangles | 1 | 2 | 3 | 4 | 5 | → | 10 |
|---|---|---|---|---|---|---|---|
| Number of matches | 3 | | | | | | |

**3**

| Number of squares | 1 | 2 | 3 | 4 | 5 | → | 10 |
|---|---|---|---|---|---|---|---|
| Number of matches | 4 | | | | | | |

**4**

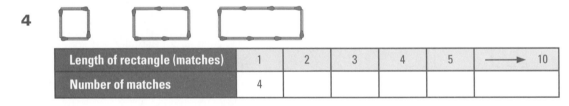

| Length of rectangle (matches) | 1 | 2 | 3 | 4 | 5 | → | 10 |
|---|---|---|---|---|---|---|---|
| Number of matches | 4 | | | | | | |

**5**

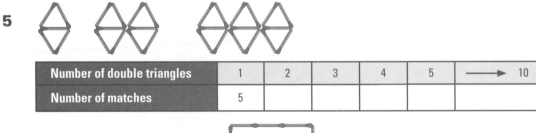

| Number of double triangles | 1 | 2 | 3 | 4 | 5 | → | 10 |
|---|---|---|---|---|---|---|---|
| Number of matches | 5 | | | | | | |

**6**

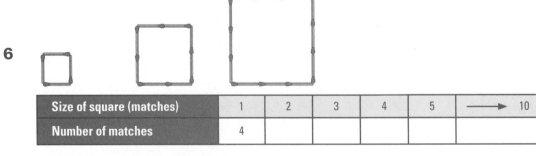

| Size of square (matches) | 1 | 2 | 3 | 4 | 5 | → | 10 |
|---|---|---|---|---|---|---|---|
| Number of matches | 4 | | | | | | |

Working Mathematically

# Hexagon puzzles

1   Kathy is making hexagons with matches. She uses 6 to make 1 hexagon, and 11 to make 2 hexagons next to each other.

**a**   How many matches will she use to make 3 hexagons next to each other?  _____

**b**   Continue the pattern of matches needed in this pattern of hexagons:

6, 11, _____ , _____ , _____ , _____ , _____

**c**   How many matches will she use to make 5 hexagons next to each other?  _____

**d**   If Kathy has 21 matches how many hexagons can she make next to each other?  _____

**e**   If Kathy has 31 matches how many hexagons can she make next to each other?  _____

2   Six people can be seated at a single hexagonal table. If two tables are placed end to end 10 people can be seated as shown in the diagram.

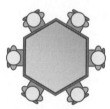 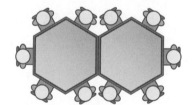 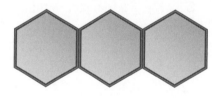

**a**   If 3 tables are placed end to end how many people can be seated?  _____

**b**   Continue the pattern of the number of people that can be seated when hexagonal tables are placed next to each other:

6, 10, _____ , _____ , _____ , _____ , _____

**c**   If 6 tables are placed end to end how many people can be seated?  _____

**d**   How many hexagonal tables must be placed end to end to seat 22 people?  _____

# Puzzles with matches

You can make two squares with

8 matches:

or 7 matches:

You can make three squares with

12 matches:

or 11 matches:

or 10 matches:

Now do the following exercises and draw your solutions on grid paper.

**1** Make 4 squares with:

    **a** 16 matches _____

    **b** 15 matches _____

    **c** 14 matches _____

    **d** 13 matches _____

    **e** 12 matches _____

**2** Make 5 squares with:

    **a** 18 matches _____

    **b** 16 matches _____

**3** Make 3 triangles with:

    **a** 9 matches _____

    **b** 7 matches _____

**4** Make 4 triangles with:

    **a** 10 matches _____

    **b** 9 matches _____

**5** Make 5 triangles with:

    **a** 12 matches

    **b** 11 matches

**6** Remove 4 matches from this figure so that 5 squares remain.

**7** From the figure below:

    **a** remove 5 matches, to leave 4 small squares;

    **b** remove 3 matches, to leave 4 squares;

    **c** remove 4 matches, to leave 3 squares;

    **d** remove 6 matches, to leave 2 squares.

See *Teacher's Book* for grid paper.

Working Mathematically

# Folding paper

**1** Take a sheet of paper.
Fold it in half. Unfold it and count
the number of small rectangles.
Refold it, then fold it in half again.
After each fold, unfold the paper
and count the number of rectangles
you have made. Continue doing
this until the paper can no longer be
folded.

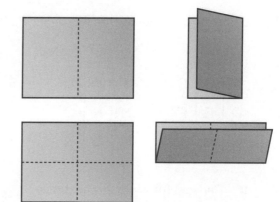

**a** Complete this table.

| Folds | 1 | 2 | 3 | 4 | 5 | 6 |
|---|---|---|---|---|---|---|
| Small rectangles | 2 | 4 | | | | |

Now experiment with paper of different sizes and thickness.

**b** What is the maximum number of folds you can make? _____

**c** Can you predict the number of small
rectangles that will be made with 8 folds? _____

**2 a** Take a long sheet of paper, and fold
it in half towards you. Refold it in half
away from you, then again in half
towards you, and so on until you can
no longer fold the paper.

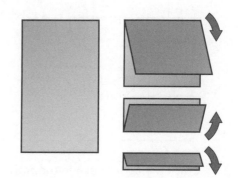

After each fold, unfold the paper and
count the number of creases on it.
As you work, complete this table.

| Folds | 1 | 2 | 3 | 4 |
|---|---|---|---|---|
| Creases | 2 | | | |
| Small rectangles | 2 | 4 | | |

**b** Can you predict the number of
rectangles that will be made with 6 folds? _____

# Secret codes

**1**  Using the code below, the word 'SECRET' would be written like this:

| A | B | C |
|---|---|---|
| D | E | F |
| G | H | I |

| J | K | L |
|---|---|---|
| M | N | O |
| P | Q | R |

| S | T | U |
|---|---|---|
| V | W | X |
| Y | Z | and |

**a**  Can you translate this sentence?

———  ——  ———  ———  ———  ———  ———  ———  ——— ——— ——  ———  ———  ——  ———

**b**  Now write 'TEACHERS HAVE CLASS', using the same code.

———  ——  ———  ———  ———  ———  ———  ———  ———  ———  ———  ———

**2**  Here is a different code. Use it to work out the message below.

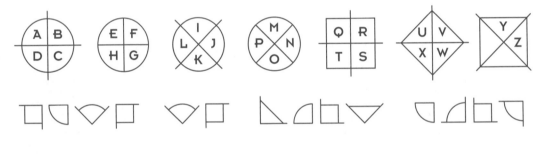

——  ———  ——  ——  ———  ——  ——  ———  ———  ——  ———  ———  ———

**3**  Crack the code! Each letter of the alphabet is represented by a number.

DIG is written as 2 7 5.

MAT is written as 11 25 18.

| A | ___ | J | ___ | S | ___ |
|---|-----|---|-----|---|-----|
| B | ___ | K | ___ | T | ___ |
| C | ___ | L | ___ | U | ___ |
| D | ___ | M | ___ | V | ___ |
| E | ___ | N | ___ | W | ___ |
| F | ___ | O | ___ | X | ___ |
| G | ___ | P | ___ | Y | ___ |
| H | ___ | Q | ___ | Z | ___ |
| I | ___ | R | ___ |   |     |

**a**  Using this secret code, write these words:

    **i**   CAT  _____

    **ii**  HUNGRY  _____

    **iii** MATHS  _____

**b**  The following message was written in the same code:

6 13 14 3   23 13 19   25 16 3   3 12 8 13 23 7 12 5   18 6 7 17

Can you translate it?  _____

# enrich-e-matics 3ʳᵈ EDITION
## BOOK 3
## ANSWERS

## Number grids (page 1)

**1** 4, 1, 5    **2** 2, 2, 7    **3** 7, 3, 4    **4** 5, 4, 3

**5** 4, 3, 6    **6** 2, 3, 5    **7** 6, 6, 4    **8** 8, 1, 5

**9** 8, 3, 4    **10** 9, 1, 5    **11** 7, 8, 9    **12** 7, 7, 6

## Grid puzzles (page 2)

**1** 3, 1, 1, 1    **2** 1, 3, 1, 4    **3** 4, 1, 2, 1    **4** 5, 5, 1, 1

**5** 1, 2, 1, 3    **6** 1, 1, 2, 4    **7** 2, 2, 2, 3    **8** 2, 4, 2, 1

                                                         3, 1, 1, 4            3, 3, 1, 2

**9** 6, 2, 1, 4    **10** 4, 1, 1, 4    **11** 5, 3, 1, 3    **12** 4, 3, 1, 2

     5, 3, 2, 3            3, 2, 2, 3           4, 4, 2, 2           3, 4, 2, 1

     4, 4, 3, 2            2, 3, 3, 2           3, 5, 3, 1

     3, 5, 4, 1            1, 4, 4, 1

## Missing numbers (page 3)

**1** 6, 12                                **2** 9, 7

**3** ÷ 2, 6, 16                 **4** + 2, 5, 8, 10

**5** − 3, 20, 18, 17           **6** − 4, 5, 15, 11

**7** × 2, 12, 3               **8** × 3, 9, 4, 36

## Number sentences (page 4)

**1** 2 + 3 + 4 = 9         **2** 6 + 5 − 2 = 9

**3** 4 + 3 − 5 = 2 or 5 + 3 − 6 = 2

**4** 6 + 3 − 5 = 4 or 6 + 2 − 4 = 4 or 5 + 3 − 4 = 4 or 5 + 2 − 3 = 4

**5** 5 + 3 + 2 = 10      **6** 5 + 4 + 2 = 11 or 6 + 3 + 2 = 11

**7** 6 − 3 − 2 = 1        **8** 6 − 4 − 2 = 0 or 5 − 3 − 2 = 0

**9** 6 − 5 + 2 = 3 or 5 − 4 + 2 = 3 or 4 − 3 + 2 = 3

**10** 2 × 3 + 4 = 10

**11** 2 × 5 − 3 = 7 or 2 × 6 − 5 = 7 or 3 × 4 − 5 = 7

**12** 2 × 4 − 6 = 2 or 2 × 3 − 4 = 2      **13** 2 × 3 − 6 = 0

**14** 2 × 4 − 5 = 3    **15** 2 × 3 + 5 = 11 or 2 × 4 + 3 = 11

## Number ideas (page 5)

**1** +, −      **2** ×, −      **3** +, −      **4** +, −

**5** ×, − or +, × or (2 + 3) × 1 = 5

**6** ×, × or +, +                 **7** ×, +      **8** +, −

**9** ×, −    **10** ×, −    **11** ×, −    **12** ×, −    **13** ×, −

**14** −, + or ×, −             **15** +, −    **16** ×, −

**17** ×, +    **18** ×, +    **19** ×, −    **20** ×, −

## Numbers and symbols (page 6)

**1** 2 + 2 − (2 × 2) = 0          2 + 2 − 2 − 2 = 0

     2 + 2 − (2 + 2) = 0         2 × 2 − 2 − 2 = 0

     2 × 2 − 2 × 2 = 0           (2 + 2) × (2 − 2) = 0

     (2 × 2) × (2 − 2) = 0        (2 + 2 − 2) ÷ 2 = 1

     (2 × 2 − 2) ÷ 2 = 1         2 ÷ 2 + 2 − 2 = 1

     2 × 2 ÷ 2 ÷ 2 = 1           2 + 2 − 2 ÷ 2 = 3

     (2 + 2 + 2) ÷ 2 = 3         (2 × 2 + 2) ÷ 2 = 3

     2 + 2 + 2 ÷ 2 = 5           2 × 2 + 2 ÷ 2 = 5

     2 + 2 + 2 + 2 = 8           2 + 2 + 2 × 2 = 8

     2 × 2 + 2 × 2 = 8           2 + 2 × 2 × 2 = 10

**2** 3 × (3 − 3) = 0             3 + 3 − 3 = 3

     3 ÷ (3 ÷ 3) = 3            3 × 3 ÷ 3 = 3

     3 + 3 ÷ 3 = 4              3 × 3 − 3 = 6

     3 + 3 + 3 = 9              3 × (3 + 3) = 18

**3** 3 + 3 − 3 − 3 = 0          3 × 3 − 3 × 3 = 0

     (3 + 3) × (3 − 3) = 0       3 × 3 × (3 − 3) = 0

     (3 × 3 − 3) ÷ 3 = 2        3 ÷ 3 + 3 ÷ 3 = 2

     3 × 3 − 3 − 3 = 3          (3 + 3 + 3) ÷ 3 = 3

     3 + 3 + 3 − 3 = 6          (3 + 3) × 3 ÷ 3 = 6

     3 × 3 + 3 − 3 = 9          3 × 3 × (3 ÷ 3) = 9

     3 × 3 × 3 ÷ 3 = 9          3 × 3 + 3 ÷ 3 = 10

## Square puzzles (page 7)

**1** A = 2    **2** A = 1    **3** A = 2    **4** A = 3    **5** A = 5

     B = 3        B = 4        B = 3        B = 1        B = 1

     C = 4        C = 3        C = 1        C = 4        C = 3

**6** A = 4    **7** A = 2    **8** A = 2    **9** A = 2    **10** A = 5

     B = 2        B = 1        B = 3        B = 3        B = 1

     C = 3        C = 3        C = 1        C = 4        C = 4

                  D = 4        D = 5        D = 5        D = 3

## Find my rule (page 8)

| | RULE | | Last box | | |
|---|---|---|---|---|---|
| 1 | − 3 | × 2 | 5 | 2 | 4 |
| 2 | + 4 | × 2 | 2 | 6 | 12 |
| 3 | × 2 | − 7 | 10 | 20 | 13 |
| 4 | + 9 | − 4 | 5 | 14 | 10 |
| 5 | − 6 | + 11 | 12 | 6 | 17 |
| 6 | × 3 | − 5 | 5 | 15 | 10 |
| 7 | − 4 | × 3 | 2 | 6 | 6 |
| 8 | × 3 | × 2 | 1 | 3 | 6 |
| 9 | + 2 | × 3 | 2 | 4 | 12 |
| 10 | − 9 | × 2 | 11 | 2 | 4 |

## What's the rule? (page 9)

| | RULE | | Last box | | |
|---|---|---|---|---|---|
| 1 | × 3 | − 4 | 8 | 24 | 20 |
| 2 | × 5 | + 2 | 4 | 20 | 22 |
| 3 | − 5 | × 3 | 6 | 1 | 3 |
| 4 | + 2 | × 5 | 6 | 8 | 40 |
| 5 | + 3 | × 10 | 7 | 10 | 100 |
| 6 | × 10 | − 7 | 6 | 60 | 53 |
| 7 | × 3 | × 2 | 4 | 12 | 24 |
| 8 | × 5 | − 11 | 4 | 20 | 9 |
| 9 | × 2 | × 5 | 4 | 8 | 40 |
| 10 | − 9 | × 3 | 12 | 3 | 9 |

## Which two numbers? (page 10)

**1 a** 1 + 4, 2 + 3
  **b** 1 + 5, 2 + 4, 3 + 3
  **c** 1 + 9, 2 + 8, 3 + 7, 4 + 6, 5 + 5
  **d** 1 + 11, 2 + 10, 3 + 9, 4 + 8, 5 + 7, 6 + 6
  **e** 1 + 14, 2 + 13, 3 + 12, 4 + 11, 5 + 10, 6 + 9, 7 + 8

**2 a** $1 \times 6, 2 \times 3$
  **b** $1 \times 12, 2 \times 6, 3 \times 4$
  **c** $1 \times 16, 2 \times 8, 4 \times 4$
  **d** $1 \times 20, 2 \times 10, 4 \times 5$
  **e** $1 \times 24, 2 \times 12, 3 \times 8, 4 \times 6$

**3 a** 4 − 1, 5 − 2, 6 − 3, 7 − 4, 8 − 5 and so on
  **b** 6 − 1, 7 − 2, 8 − 3, 9 − 4, 10 − 5 and so on
  **c** 7 − 1, 8 − 2, 9 − 3, 10 − 4, 11 − 5 and so on
  **d** 11 − 1, 12 − 2, 13 − 3, 14 − 4, 15 − 5 and so on
  **e** 18 − 1, 19 − 2, 20 − 3, 21 − 4, 22 − 5 and so on

## Find two numbers (page 11)

| | | | | |
|---|---|---|---|---|
| **1** 2, 5 | **2** 2, 8 | **3** 3, 7 | **4** 1, 9 | **5** 2, 7 |
| **6** 1, 8 | **7** 2, 5 | **8** 1, 7 | **9** 3, 5 | **10** 5, 6 |
| **11** 4, 8 | **12** 2, 10 | **13** 2, 3 | **14** 3, 5 | **15** 2, 6 |
| **16** 5, 7 | **17** 5, 6 | **18** 7, 8 | **19** 9, 6 | **20** 3, 6 |
| **21** 6, 12 | **22** 10, 20 | **23** 7, 14 | **24** 9, 18 | |

## Number puzzles (page 12)

**1 a**, **b**, **c**

**2 a**, **b**, **c**, **d**

**3** $9 - 7 = 2$, $\times 4$, $8 - 3 = 5$

**4** $8 - 6 = 2$, $\div 7$, $1 + 4 = 5$ or $5 - 3 = 2$, $\div 4$, $1 + 7 = 8$

## Magic squares (page 13)

**1 a**
| 8 | 1 | 6 |
|---|---|---|
| 3 | 5 | 7 |
| 4 | 9 | 2 |

**b**
| 6 | 7 | 2 |
|---|---|---|
| 1 | 5 | 9 |
| 8 | 3 | 4 |

**c**
| 4 | 3 | 8 |
|---|---|---|
| 9 | 5 | 1 |
| 2 | 7 | 6 |

**2 a**
| 7 | 0 | 5 |
|---|---|---|
| 2 | 4 | 6 |
| 3 | 8 | 1 |

**b**
| 1 | 8 | 3 |
|---|---|---|
| 6 | 4 | 2 |
| 5 | 0 | 7 |

**c**
| 3 | 2 | 7 |
|---|---|---|
| 8 | 4 | 0 |
| 1 | 6 | 5 |

**3 a**
| 9 | 2 | 7 |
|---|---|---|
| 4 | 6 | 8 |
| 5 | 10 | 3 |

**b**
| 7 | 8 | 3 |
|---|---|---|
| 2 | 6 | 10 |
| 9 | 4 | 5 |

**c**
| 5 | 4 | 9 |
|---|---|---|
| 10 | 6 | 2 |
| 3 | 8 | 7 |

## Patterns and sequences (page 14)

| | | Pattern | | | Pattern |
|---|---|---|---|---|---|
| **1** | 10, 12, 14 | +2 | **2** | 11, 13, 15 | + 2 |
| **3** | 23, 27, 31 | + 4 | **4** | 30, 37, 44 | + 7 |
| **5** | 50, 60, 70 | + 10 | **6** | 25, 30, 35 | + 5 |
| **7** | 23, 26, 29 | + 3 | **8** | 45, 55, 65 | + 10 |
| **9** | 33, 41, 49 | + 8 | **10** | 29, 31, 33 | + 2 |
| **11** | 10, 5, 0 | − 5 | **12** | 42, 40, 38 | − 2 |
| **13** | 50, 40, 30 | − 10 | **14** | 11, 8, 5 | − 3 |
| **15** | 26, 22, 18 | − 4 | **16** | 28, 23, 18 | − 5 |
| **17** | 20, 24, 28 | + 4 | **18** | 35, 42, 49 | + 7 |
| **19** | 10, 8, 6 | − 2 | **20** | 56, 67, 78 | + 11 |
| **21** | 15, 18, 21 | + 3 | **22** | 30, 36, 42 | + 6 |
| **23** | 37, 46, 55 | + 9 | **24** | 53, 44, 35 | − 9 |
| **25** | 35, 28, 21 | − 7 | **26** | 29, 23, 17 | − 6 |
| **27** | 86, 98, 110 | + 12 | **28** | 60, 45, 30 | − 15 |
| **29** | 59, 72, 85 | + 13 | **30** | 56, 45, 34 | − 11 |

## Missing numbers (page 15)

| | | | | | | | |
|---|---|---|---|---|---|---|---|
| **1** | 9 | (+ 3) | **2** | 18 | (− 3) | **3** 50 | (− 5) |
| **4** | 89 | (− 4) | **5** | 33 | (+ 4) | **6** 67 | (+ 11) |

**7** 16 (+ 1, + 2, + 3, + 4, + 5 + 6, + 7)
**8** 15 (− 1, − 2, − 3, − 4, − 5, − 6, − 7)
**9** 74 (+ 2, + 3, + 4, + 5, + 6, + 7)
**10** 91 (− 1, − 2, − 3, − 4, − 5, − 6)
**11** 15 (+ 2, + 3, + 4, + 5, + 6, + 7, + 8)
**12** 12 (+ 3, − 1, + 3, − 1, + 3, − 1 + 3, − 1 or 2 patterns 6, 8, 10, 12, 14 and 9, 11, 13, 15)
**13** 30 (2 patterns 2, 4, 6, 8, 10 and 10, 20, 30, 40)
**14** 7 (2 patterns 1, 3, 5, 7, 9 and 5, 10, 15, 20)
**15** 13 (2 patterns 3, 8, 13, 18, 23 and 10, 12, 14, 16)
**16** 21 (+ 6, − 2, − 6, − 2, + 6, − 2, + 6, − 2 or 2 patterns 3, 7, 11, 15, 19 and 9, 13, 17, 21)
**17** 77 (2 patterns 97, 87, 77, 67, 57 and 95, 90, 85, 80)
**18** 36 (2 patterns 28, 29, 30, 31, 32 and 36, 35, 34, 33)
**19** 29 (2 patterns 39, 34, 29, 24, 19 and 7, 10, 13, 16)
**20** 46 (2 patterns 73, 64, 55, 46, 37 and 1, 5, 9, 13)

## Find three numbers (page 16)

**1** 5, 3, 2    **2** 3, 4, 6    **3** 3, 7, 5
**4** 6, 8, 2    **5** 3, 4, 9    **6** 6, 2, 10
**7** 11, 6, 5    **8** 4, 9, 12    **9** 7, 13, 3
**10** 6, 11, 8

## Which three numbers? (page 17)

**1** 7, 6, 4    **2** 9, 10, 5    **3** 12, 3, 21
**4** 4, 1, 2    **5** 1, 3, 9    **6** 4, 8, 2
**7** 3, 8, 2    **8** 6, 5, 3    **9** 3, 8, 4
**10** 3, 5, 9

## Arrange the numbers (page 18)

There are several other solutions as the triangles can be rotated.

**1**  a 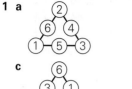  b

c   d

**2**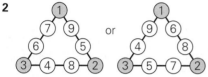

**3**  a   b

**4**  a 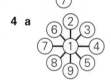  b   c

## What's the value? (page 19)

## What's the question? (page 20)

The numbers given here are only some of the possible solutions—there are many, many more.

**1**  a  7 + 1, 6 + 2, 5 + 3, 4 + 4

  b  3 + 2 + 2 + 1, 4 + 2 + 1 + 1, 3 + 3 + 1 + 1, 5 + 1 + 1 + 1

  c  9 − 1, 10 − 2, 11 − 3, 12 − 4, 20 − 12

  d  2 × 3 + 7 − 1 − 4, 10 × 2 + 5 − 9 − 8, 5 + 4 + 3 + 2 − 6

  e  For example, share 32 sweets among 4 children;
  *or* 16 ÷ 2, 24 ÷ 3, 40 ÷ 5

  f  $\frac{1}{2} \times 16$, $\frac{1}{3} \times 24$, $\frac{1}{5} \times 40$, $\frac{1}{10} \times 80$, $\frac{2}{5} \times 20$, $\frac{1}{4} \times 32$, $\frac{1}{6} \times 48$

**2**  a
| 10 | 11 | 12 | 13 | 14 | 15 | 16 | 17 |
|----|----|----|----|----|----|----|----|
| + 8 | + 7 | + 6 | + 5 | + 4 | + 3 | + 2 | + 1 |
| 18 | 18 | 18 | 18 | 18 | 18 | 18 | 18 |

  b
| 11 | 12 | 13 | 14 | 15 | 16 | 17 | 18 | 19 |
|----|----|----|----|----|----|----|----|----|
| + 9 | + 8 | + 7 | + 6 | + 5 | + 4 | + 3 | + 2 | + 1 |
| 20 | 20 | 20 | 20 | 20 | 20 | 20 | 20 | 20 |

  c
| 23 | 22 | 21 | 20 | 19 | 18 | 17 | 16 | 15 |
|----|----|----|----|----|----|----|----|----|
| + 1 | + 2 | + 3 | + 4 | + 5 | + 6 | + 7 | + 8 | + 9 |
| 24 | 24 | 24 | 24 | 24 | 24 | 24 | 24 | 24 |

**3**
| 34 | 31 | 43 | 13 | 21 | 24 | 12 | 42 |
|----|----|----|----|----|----|----|----|
| + 21 | + 24 | + 12 | + 42 | + 34 | + 31 | + 43 | + 13 |
| 55 | 55 | 55 | 55 | 55 | 55 | 55 | 55 |

**4**
| 65 | 64 | 56 | 46 | 34 | 35 | 43 | 53 |
|----|----|----|----|----|----|----|----|
| + 34 | + 35 | + 43 | + 53 | + 65 | + 64 | + 56 | + 46 |
| 99 | 99 | 99 | 99 | 99 | 99 | 99 | 99 |

## Past numbers (page 21)

**1**  a  i  3  ii  20  iii  11  iv  33  v  15

  b  i  ＶＶＶＶ  ii  ＜ＶＶＶ

  iii  ＜＜ＶＶＶＶＶＶ

  iv  ＜＜＜  v  ＜＜＜＜ＶＶＶＶＶＶ

**2**  a  i  4  ii  6  iii  12  iv  15  v  19

  b  i  ● ●  ii  •̲ •̲  iii  ●●●●  iv  ̲•̲  v  •̳

## Continue the pattern (page 22)

**1**  5 × 9 = 50 − 5
6 × 9 = 60 − 6

**2**  5 × 8 = 50 − 10
6 × 8 = 60 − 12

**3**  1 + 2 + 3 + 4 + 5 + 6 + 5 + 4 + 3 + 2 + 1 = 6 × 6
1 + 2 + 3 + 4 + 5 + 6 + 7 + 6 + 5 + 4 + 3 + 2 + 1 = 7 × 7

**4**  1 + 2 + 3 + 4 + 5 = 6 + 7 + 8 + 9 + 10 − 5 × 5
1 + 2 + 3 + 4 + 5 + 6 = 7 + 8 + 9 + 10 + 11 + 12 − 6 × 6

**5**  16 + 17 + 18 + 19 + 20 = 21 + 22 + 23 + 24
25 + 26 + 27 + 28 + 29 + 30 = 31 + 32 + 33 + 34 + 35

**6**  (5 − 4) × (5 + 4) = 9 = 5 + 4
(6 − 5) × (6 + 5) = 11 = 6 + 5

**7**  (5 − 1) × (5 + 1) = 24
(6 − 1) × (6 + 1) = 35

**8**  (5 − 3) × (5 + 3) = 2 × 8
(6 − 4) × (6 + 4) = 2 × 10

## Shapes and values (page 23)

**1**  ④, △5, ▨3, ▭7

**2**  ▭7, ○2, △3, ⬠8

**3**  △5, ○1, ▨3, ▱8, ⬡7

**4**  ○3, ⬡7, ▨2, △9, ▭4

**5**  ▭2, ○1, ⬡7, △5, ▨3

**6**  ▭5, ▭8, ⬡3, ⬡7, △1

**7**  ▭3, ○4, ⬡7, ▨2, △5

**8**  ⬡1, ▨3, ○2, ▱9, △4

**9**  ▭2, △4, ▨9, ○5, ⬡1

**10**  ▭5, ▨6, △4, ○3, ⬡1

## Related rows (page 24)

| | | Rule | | | Rule | | | Rule |
|---|---|------|---|---|------|---|---|------|
| **1** | 11 | + 5 | **2** | 4 | × 2 | **3** | 4 | − 8 |
| **4** | 50 | × 10 | **5** | 8 | × 4 | **6** | 15 | + 6 |
| **7** | 5 | × 5 | **8** | 12 | × 2 | **9** | 13 | × 2 + 1 |
| **10** | 3 | × 2 − 1 | **11** | 49 | × 10 − 1 | **12** | 9 | × 5 − 1 |
| **13** | 24 | × 4 | **14** | 25 | × 4 + 1 | **15** | 7 | × 3 + 1 |
| **16** | 16 | × 5 + 1 | **17** | 16 | square | **18** | 15 | square − 1 |
| **19** | 3 | − 5 | **20** | 26 | square + 1 | | | |

## Differences (page 25)

**1** 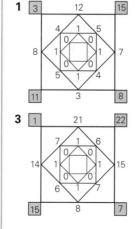  **2**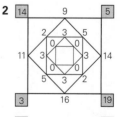

**3**  **4**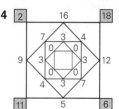

C

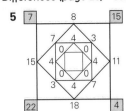

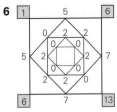

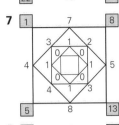

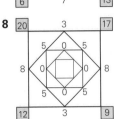

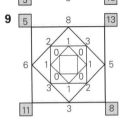

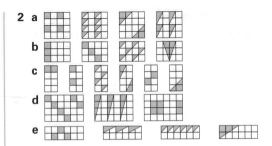

## Number line (page 26)

| | | | |
|---|---|---|---|
| **1** 17 | **2** 170 | **3** 1700 | **4** 147 |
| **5** 227 | **6** 1170 | **7** 464 | **8** 31 |

## Find the value (page 27)

| | | | | |
|---|---|---|---|---|
| **1** = 5 | **2** = 50 | **3** = 60 | **4** = 20 | **5** = 9 |
| **6** = 12 | **7** = 25 | **8** = 300 | **9** = 75 | **10** = 150 |

## Counting-frame arithmetic (page 28)

**1 a** 2   **b** 200   **c** 200   **d** 101

**2 a** 12   **b** 12   **c** 3   **d** 300

 **e** 30   **f** 300   **g** 201

**3 a** 4   **b** 13   **c** 22   **d** 31

 **e** 40   **f** 103   **g** 112   **h** 121

 **i** 130   **j** 202   **k** 211   **l** 220

 **m** 301   **n** 310   **o** 400

## Shading parts (page 29)

**1** There are a very large number of solutions. Please remember that this is only a sample.

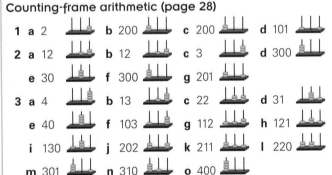

**a**

**b**

**c**

**d**

**e**

## What fraction's shaded? (page 30)

There are many possible solutions.

**1** $\frac{1}{2}$   **2** $\frac{1}{2}$   **3** $\frac{1}{2}$   **4** $\frac{1}{4}$   **5** $\frac{1}{2}$

**6** $\frac{3}{8}$   **7** $\frac{1}{2}$   **8** $\frac{3}{8}$   **9** $\frac{1}{2}$   **10** $\frac{5}{8}$

## How old? (page 31)

**1** 8   **2** 24   **3** 11

**4** Brenda 8, Jacob 4, Tammy 10

**5** 6   **6** 5   **7** Lydia 7, Yvonne 8, Greg 14

## Coins (page 32)

**1** 20c, 40c, 60c, 5c, 25c, 45c, 65c

**2** 10c, 20c, 30c, 40c, 50c, 5c, 15c, 25c, 35c, 45c, 55c

**3** 20c, 40c, 50c, 70c, 90c

**4** 10c, 50c, 60c, $1, $1.10, $1.50, $1.60, $2, $2.10

**5** 10c, 20c, 50c, 60c, 70c, $1, $1.10, $1.20, $1.50, $1.60, $1.70

## Money problems (page 33)

**1** 5   **2** 8

**3** Expressing the answer as a table, and working systematically, will help to make sure that all possible ways are found.

| 20c | 10c | 5c |
|---|---|---|
| 2 | – | – |
| 1 | 2 | – |
| 1 | 1 | 2 |
| 1 | 0 | 4 |
| – | 4 | – |
| – | 3 | 2 |
| – | 2 | 4 |
| – | 1 | 6 |
| – | – | 8 |

**4 a** $3.00   **b** 75c   **c** $2.25

**5 a** $2.40   **b** $3.60

 **c** 40c   **d** 80c

**6** $1.50   **7** $8

**8 a** 6 lollies, 10c change

 **b** 4 biscuits, 12c change

## How much money? (page 34)

**1 a** 18   **b** 7   **c** 27

**2 a** 40c   **b** 50c

**3** $5.90

| | Week 1 | Week 2 | Week 3 | Week 4 | Total |
|---|---|---|---|---|---|
| Spent | $1.80 | 70c | $2.10 | $1.50 | |
| Saved | $1.20 | $2.30 | $0.90 | $1.50 | $5.90 |

**4 a** 50c + 20c + 20c, 50c + 20c + 10c + 10c

 **b** $1 + 50c + 10c, $1 + 20c + 20c + 10c + 10c, 50c + 50c + 20c + 20c + 10c + 10c

**5** $1.60

## Missing shapes (page 35)

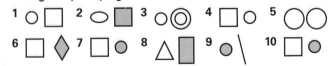

## Patterns with squares (page 36)

 1    2    3    4

 5   6   7

8

| | 1st shape | 2nd shape | 3rd shape | 4th shape | 5th shape |
|---|---|---|---|---|---|
| 1 | 2 | 4 | 6 | 8 | 10 |
| 2 | 1 | 3 | 5 | 7 | 9 |
| 3 | 1 | 4 | 7 | 10 | 13 |
| 4 | 1 | 4 | 9 | 16 | 25 |
| 5 | 3 | 6 | 10 | 15 | 21 |
| 6 | 1 | 3 | 6 | 10 | 15 |
| 7 | 8 | 12 | 16 | 20 | 24 |

## Faces (page 37)

1

2

## Building blocks (page 38)

1
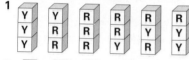

2

## Shading circles (page 39)

1   2
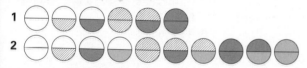

## Shading sectors (page 40)

1

2   6 patterns:
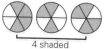

4 white   1 shaded   2 shaded   3 shaded   4 shaded

3
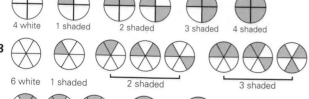

6 white   1 shaded   2 shaded   3 shaded

4 shaded   5 shaded   6 shaded

## Colour these flags (page 41)

1
| R | R | B | B | Y | Y |
|---|---|---|---|---|---|
| B | Y | Y | R | R | B |
| Y | B | R | Y | B | R |

2 Altogether there are 27 possible colour combinations. Given here are the remaining 24.

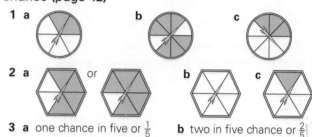

3

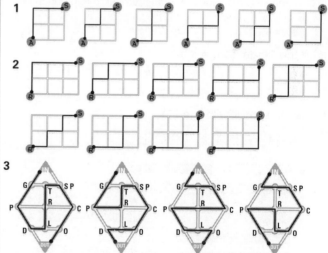

## Chance (page 42)

1 a   b   c

2 a   or   b   c

3 a one chance in five or $\frac{1}{5}$   b two in five chance or $\frac{2}{5}$
  c three in five chance or $\frac{3}{5}$   d zero

4 yellow, green, red, blue

## How many routes? (page 43)

1

2

3

## Vegetable patch (page 44)

1

| Front | |
|---|---|
| P | C |
| Z | T |
| O | L |
| M | S |
| Back | |

2 There are many different ways to describe the position of the flowers in this garden. Your teacher can check your work.

## Graphs (page 45)

1 a between 2 p.m. and 3 p.m.
  b between noon and 1 p.m.

E

**c** 40        **d** between 11 a.m. and noon

**e** 10 a.m.–11 a.m. and 1 p.m.–2 p.m.

**f** 70        **g** 320        **h** $640

**2**

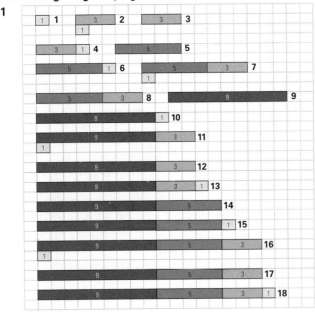

## Working with graphs (page 46)

**1 a** 5 cm        **b** 20 cm        **c** 30 cm

**2 a** 30        **b** 15

**3 a** 24        **b** 48

## Temperature readings (page 47)

**1 a** 25        **b** 26        **c** 24        **d** 29

**2 a** 31        **b** 33        **c** 30        **d** 30

**3 a** 32        **b** 30        **c** 33        **d** 32

## Temperature challenges (page 48)

**1 a** 10 a.m. to 11 a.m.  **b** 11 a.m. to noon  **c** 12°C

**d** 14°C        **e** 8°C        **f** 9 a.m.

**2 a** 11 a.m.        **b** highest 26°C and lowest 18°C

**c** 23°C        **d** between 10 a.m. and 11 a.m.

**e** 9 a.m. and 1 p.m.

**f** Between 8 a.m. and 9 a.m. the temperature rose 2°C.
Between 9 a.m. and 10 a.m. the temperature rose 2°C.
Between 10 a.m. and 11 a.m. the temperature rose 4°C.
Between 11 a.m. and 1 p.m. the temperature dropped 6°C.
Between 1 p.m. and 3 p.m. the temperature rose 2°C.
Between 3 p.m. and 4 p.m. the temperature didn't change.

## Find the length (page 49)

**1 a** 6 cm        **b** 9 cm        **c** 4 cm        **d** 5 cm

**2 a** 7 cm, 2 cm        **b** 13 cm, 4 cm        **c** 7 cm, 9 cm

## Measuring lengths (page 50)

**1**

## 2

| | |
|---|---|
| 2 = 3 − 1 | 17 = 15 + 3 − 1 |
| 4 = 3 + 1 | 18 = 15 + 3 |
| 8 = 7 + 1 | 19 = 15 + 1 + 1 |
| 9 = 7 + 3 − 1 | 20 = 15 + 7 + 1 − 3 |
| 10 = 7 + 3 | 21 = 15 + 7 − 1 |
| 11 = 7 + 3 + 1 | 22 = 15 + 7 |
| 12 = 15 − 3 | 23 = 15 + 7 + 1 |
| 13 = 15 + 1 − 3 | 24 = 15 + 7 + 3 − 1 |
| 14 = 15 − 1 | 25 = 15 + 7 + 3 |
| 16 = 15 + 1 | 26 = 15 + 7 + 3 + 1 |

## How many tiles? (page 51)

**1** 32        **2 a** 30        **b** 22        **c** 26

## Time puzzles (page 52)

**1 a** Monday        **b** Monday        **c** Wednesday

**2 a** Friday        **b** Friday        **c** Friday

**3 a** 90 minutes        **b** 195 minutes

**4 a** 10:20 a.m.   **b** 7:45 a.m.   **c** 1 hour 40 minutes

**5 a** dressed: 7:17        **b** breakfast eaten: 7:26

**c** room cleaned: 7:32   **d** clarinet practised: 7:57

**e** school reached: 8:17   **f** 13 minutes

**6 a** 1 October        **b** 5 November

## Time challenges (page 53)

**1 a** February, March, July, September

**b** Saturday, Sunday, Tuesday, Wednesday

**c** summer, autumn, winter, spring

**2 a** 11:59        **b** 12:03        **c** 11:48

**3 a** 145 seconds        **b** 1 min 50 secs

**4 a** 270 m        **b** 60 litres

**5** 23 min        **6** 10:45 a.m.

**7 a** 15 sec + 45 sec
15 sec + 15 sec + 30 sec
15 sec + 15 sec + 15 sec + 15 sec

**b** 45 sec + 45 sec
45 sec + 15 sec + 30 sec
30 sec + 30 sec + 15 sec + 15 sec
45 sec + 15 sec + 15 sec + 15 sec
30 sec + 15 sec + 15 sec + 15 sec + 15 sec
15 sec + 15 sec + 15 sec + 15 sec + 15 sec + 15 sec

## Train timetable (page 54)

**1** 21 minutes        **2** 11 minutes        **3** 25 minutes

**4 a** 7 minutes        **b** 7:47

**5** 7:15        **6** 13 minutes

## Read the dial (page 55)

**1 a** 20 L        **b** 10 L        **c** 30 L

**2 a** 30 L        **b** 15 L        **c** 20 L

**3 a** 18 L        **b** 60 L        **c** 27 L

**4 a** 25 L        **b** 25 L        **c** 75 L

## Weighing parcels (page 56)

**1** 14 kg, 2 kg, 8 kg        **2** 13 kg, 7 kg, 3 kg

**3** 18 kg, 3 kg, 5 kg        **4** 11 kg, 3 kg, 5 kg

## Mass problem solving (page 57)

**1** 21 kg, 17 kg, 38 kg        **2** 24 kg, 27 kg, 51 kg

**3** 8 kg, 2 kg, 10 kg        **4** 7 kg, 10 kg, 17 kg

**5** 200 g, 300 g, 500g        **6** 350 g, 250 g, 600 g

**7** 0.2 kg = 200 g, 1.8 kg = 1800 g, 2 kg = 2000 g

## Find the mass (page 58)

**1** 650 g           **2** 450 g
**3** 3.7 kg or 3 kg 700 g    **4** 850 g
**5** 1.65 kg or 1 kg 650 g    **6** 2.45 kg or 2 kg 450 g

## Travelling (page 59)

**1 a** 35 km    **b** 18 km
    **c** Charring Cross
**2 a** 7    **b** level 1
    **c** level 2

**d**
> Charring Cross | White City
> 22 km    13 km
> ←      →

## Count the shapes (page 60)

**1 a** 2   **b** 4   **c** 6   **d** 6   **e** 9   **f** 4
**2 a** 4   **b** 5   **c** 6   **d** 8   **e** 3
**3 a** 3   **b** 4   **c** 2   **d** 2   **e** 6   **f** 4
   **g** 5   **h** 6

## Counting cubes (page 61)

**1 a** 6   **b** 9   **c** 6   **d** 9   **e** 8   **f** 18
   **g** 24   **h** 18   **i** 6   **j** 12   **k** 9   **l** 18
**2 a** 9   **b** 6   **c** 7

## Packing boxes (page 62)

**1 a** l = 16 cm    w = 9 cm    h = 4 cm
   **b** l = 12 cm    w = 8 cm    h = 9 cm
**2 a** 48                   **b** 6

## Rolling boxes (page 63)

**1**        **2**
**3**        **4**
**5**        **6**

## Torn rectangles (page 64)

**1** 8    **2** 12    **3** 14    **4** 15
**5** 18    **6** 9    **7** 20    **8** 18

## Position (page 65)

**1 a** G8, G9, G10, G11, G12 or E6, E7, E8, E9, E10
   **b** G13        **c** F10, F11, F12, F13
**2** [★ ○ △ ●]     **3** 11
                  **4** Niva, Joel, Gabriel, Asher and Emma

## Tessellations (page 66)

These tessellations can be coloured in two different ways.

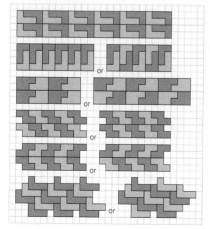

## Solid shapes (page 67)

**1 A** rectangular prism    **B** square pyramid
   **C** hexagonal prism    **D** cylinder
   **E** cube             **F** triangular prism
   **G** pentagonal pyramid    **H** cone
**2 a** D   **b** C   **c** H   **d** G   **e** F   **f** G
**3** 6        **4** 12        **5** 5

## Bearings (page 68)

**1 a** east    **b** south    **c** north
**2 a** 3 blocks south    **b** 5 blocks east
   **c** 3 blocks south then 3 blocks west, or 3 blocks west then 3 blocks south
     AND 1 block south then 5 blocks east, or 5 blocks east then 1 block south
   **d** 4 blocks south then 3 blocks east, or 3 blocks east then 4 blocks south
   **e** 4 blocks south then 2 blocks west, or 2 blocks west then 4 blocks south

## Challenging cubes (page 69)

**1 a** ▢    **b** ☀    **c** ★
   **d**     **e**
**2 a** ☆ ● ○ ⬡ ◆    **b** ○ ⊙ ◆ ● ☆
   **c** ○

## Painting solids (page 70)

**1** 4, 2, 6    **2** 4, 4, 1, 9    **3** 4, 6, 2, 12    **4** 8, 12, 4, 24

## How many blocks? (page 71)

**1 a** 18    **b** 12    **c** 60
**2 a** 24    **b** 8    **c** 32

## Amazing mathematics (page 72)

**1** The result is always 4.
**2** The result is always the number you originally thought of.
**3** The result is always 5.

## Logic using scales (page 73)

**1** 2   **2** 4   **3** 2   **4** 3   **5** 2   **6** 5
**7** 1   **8** 2   **9** 3   **10** 4   **11** 4   **12** 3

## Balanced scales (page 74)

**1** 6   **2** 9   **3** 4   **4** 5   **5** 4
**6** 2   **7** 2   **8** 3   **9** 2   **10** 4

## Shapes and symbols (page 75)

**1**    **2**    **3**
**4**    **5**    **6**
**7**    **8**

## How many? (page 76)

**1** 39    **2** 48    **3** 31    **4** 26    **5** 55    **6** 40

## Shaded figures (page 77)
The values of the large squares are:

**1** 32    **2** 48    **3** 45    **4** 108    **5** 128
**6** 32    **7** 48    **8** 128    **9** 84    **10** 36
**11** 50    **12** 81    **13** 24    **14** 24    **15** 27

## Shaded values (page 78)
The values of the large squares are:

**1** 32    **2** 64    **3** 40    **4** 32    **5** 18
**6** 60    **7** 16    **8** 24    **9** 56    **10** 80
**11** 80    **12** 42    **13** 72    **14** 48    **15** 48

## Triangular numbers (page 79)

**1** 15, 21, 28, 36, 45

**2**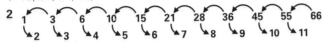

**3 a** 4 = 6, 5 = 10, 6 = 15, 7 = 21, 8 = 28, 9 = 36, 10 = 45, 11 = 55

**b** 7 members    **c** 11 members

## Joining the dots (page 80)

**1** 5 = 10, 6 = 15, 7 = 21, 8 = 28, 9 = 36

**2 a** 5    **b** 15 ⬟✦

## How many triangles? (page 81)

**1**

| Folds | 0 | 1 | 2 | 3 | 4 | 5 | 6 | 7 | 8 |
|---|---|---|---|---|---|---|---|---|---|
| Triangles | 1 | 3 | 6 | 10 | 15 | 21 | 28 | 36 | 45 |

**2** 45

## Count the triangles (page 82)

**1**

| Single | 6 |
|---|---|
| Double | 3 |
| Triple | 6 |
| Large | 1 |
| **Total** | **16** |

**2**

| Single | 8 |
|---|---|
| Double | 8 |
| Large | 2 |
| **Total** | **18** |

**3**

| Single | 6 |
|---|---|
| Double | 3 |
| Triple | 6 |
| Large | 1 |
| **Total** | **16** |

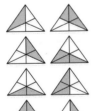

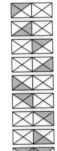

## Logic with figures (page 83)

**1**     **2**     **3**     **4**     **5**

**6**     **7**     **8**     **9**     **10**

## Matchstick puzzles (page 84)

**Rule**

**1** 8, 12, 16, 20, ➔ 40        4 × ◇
**2** 6, 9, 12, 15, ➔ 30        3 × △
**3** 8, 12, 16, 20, ➔ 40        4 × □
**4** 6, 8, 10, 12, ➔ 22        2 × ▭ + 2
**5** 10, 15, 20, 25, ➔ 50        5 × ◈
**6** 8, 12, 16, 20, ➔ 40        4 × sides of □

## Hexagon puzzles (page 85)

**1 a** 16        **b** 6, 11, 16, 21, 26, 31, 36
**c** 26        **d** 4        **e** 6
**2 a** 14        **b** 6, 10, 14, 18, 22, 26, 30
**c** 26        **d** 5

## Puzzles with matches (page 86)

**1 a** ▢▢▢▢    **b** ▢▢▢▯    **c** ▢▢▢ or ▯▢▢▢
**d** ▢▢▢▢    **e** (square grid)

**2 a** ▢▢▢▢ or ▢▢▢▢
**b** ▢▢▢▢▢ or (shape) or (shape)

**3 a** △△△△        **b** △△

**4 a** ▽▽ or △ △        **b** △△ or △△ or △

**5 a** △△◇ or △△ △ or △△△ △ or △△ △
**b** ▱△ or △△△ or other shapes

**6** (square shape)    **7 a** (shape)    **b** (shape) or (shape)
**c** (shape)    **d** (shape)

## Folding paper (page 87)

**1 a** 8, 16, 32, 64, 128, 256
Continue the pattern to predict the results of 7 and 8 folds.

**b** The maximum number of times that a sheet of paper can be folded is 8. However, depending on the size and thickness of the paper, it may be possible to fold it only 6 or 7 times.

**c** 256

**2 a**

| Folds | 1 | 2 | 3 | 4 | 5 | 6 |
|---|---|---|---|---|---|---|
| Creases | 1 | 3 | 7 | 15 | 31 | 63 |
| Rectangles | 2 | 4 | 8 | 16 | 32 | 64 |

**b** 64

## Secret codes (page 88)

**1 a** HOLIDAYS ARE FUN
**b** (coded symbols)
**2** THIS IS VERY HARD
**3** A – 25    B – 26    C – 1    D – 2    E – 3    F – 4
G – 5    H – 6    I – 7    J – 8    K – 9    L – 10
M – 11    N – 12    O – 13    P – 14    Q – 15    R – 16
S – 17    T – 18    U – 19    V – 20    W – 21    X – 22
Y – 23    Z – 24

**a i** 1 25 18    **ii** 6 19 12 5 16 23    **iii** 11 25 18 6 17
**b** HOPE YOU ARE ENJOYING THIS